To Surge with a [?] from the auth.

FIFTY YEARS IN FILMS
© John Burder 2009

First published in Britain 2009

The right of John Burder to be identified as the
author of this work has been asserted by him
in accordance with the Copyright, Designs and
Patents Act 1988.

All rights reserved. No part of this publication may be
reproduced, stored in a retrieval system or transmitted in
any form or by any means, electronic, mechanical, photocopying,
recording or otherwise without the prior permission
of the copyright owner

ISBN 978-0-9523890-6-4

Published by Big Ben Books
Email: bigbenbook@aol.com

for
GMB and CVB
with love and thanks

1. PRE – PRODUCTION

We were soaked to the skin after standing for hours in the rain on a deserted railway line in the depths of the country. Eight actors and a twenty man film crew with an ancient steam train and two veteran cars. As the director responsible this particular epic it had been my decision to shoot on a day when anyone sane would have stayed indoors. We had arrived at dawn. On paper the scene we had to shoot looked simple enough but things had not gone according to plan. The first takes were ruined when veteran cars failed to perform. Take three looked good until a jumbo jet passed overhead, ruining the period scene we are trying to reproduce, and it had gone downhill from there. As we prepared to try again I looked down at the actress who had spent the last two hours tied to the track in driving rain with mugs of whisky and soup to keep her alive between takes. She had behaved heroically but was clearly now getting concerned. As I tried to reassure her she looked up the track to the point where a seventy year old train was preparing to steam towards us. If everything went according to plan, on my cue it would screech to a halt at a point which from our carefully chosen camera position would appear to be inches away.

"It will stop won't it?" my shivering actress asked with an understandable tremor in her voice. I did not have the heart to tell her what the train driver had said when I had asked him the same question.

"Well let's put it this way", he had said sucking on his pipe.

"She is an old lady and like all old ladies she has a mind of her own, but if I manage to hit the right levers at the right points she should be alright."

I stepped back, prayed and called for action. What happened next is described later in this book.

Several years later I recalled that day when I was

lunching with a Hollywood star who was to become a good friend. We were sitting in the garden of his house in the south of on France. It had once belonged to Charlie Chaplin. I was there to discuss a television programme which he would star in and I would direct.

Sun shimmered on the swimming pool and in the distance expensive yachts cruised round the bay. Niven was at the peak of his career. His book *THE MOON'S A BALLOON* was an international best- seller and he was one of the most sought after people in film and television. He was a welcoming host and a delight to be with.

A bottle of wine was opened as soon as I arrived and we stood together, looking out across the bay. A fisherman stood on a small headland.

"Does he catch anything?" I enquired.

"Plenty!" David replied "People think he's a fishing but he is actually a Customs Inspector. He stands there all day and notes every boat that enters the harbour."

It was one of many interesting things I learned that day. It seemed a crime to discuss business in such a lovely setting so I asked David what it felt like being the author of a book which for nearly a year had been a best-seller on both sides of the Atlantic. With characteristic modesty he explained that he felt he had merely recorded what had happened in his life and was agreeably surprised that others seemed to have enjoyed what he had said.

"Anyone can do it," he insisted and then he added –

"You were telling me about filming that train. You have had an interesting life. Write it down! If it's about films people will love it."

The advice, like the man who gave it, was completely genuine. There was just one point he appeared to have missed. His films cost millions and won Oscars. I had spent years making television programmes on the sort of budgets his Producers would spend on a good lunch. David laughed and said he would like to hear about it, so I started to tell him. For a long time we talked and laughed, discussing our experiences of an industry which, whilst nominally the same, is far more diverse than most people realise.

"You must write it down," he insisted as my colleagues arrived to start the business of the day.

"Most people would love to have lead a life like yours." As I prepared to leave his house at the end of the day David thrust a large brown paper parcel into my hand and asked me to deliver it to an address in London. As I knew I had a poor reputation for leaving things on aircraft, I thought I should ask if it was valuable or not.

"Not particularly," he replied and then quietly added "But try not to lose it as I don't really want to have to do it all again."

The following day, when I arrived in London, I Discovered what the parcel contained. It was part of the handwritten manuscript for what was to become his next bestseller - BRING ON THE EMPTY HORSES. Entrusting that package to me was one of the nicest compliments I have ever been paid.

Thirty years later I eventually got round to acting on the advice I had been given on that enjoyable day in the south of France. I jotted down a few chapters and ran off some copies to give to friends attending my fortieth birthday party. I did not think much about it. A few weeks later I got a call from a BBC Presenter who had managed to get a copy of my notes. He asked if I would be prepared to" come into the studio and say a few words." I accepted his invitation and for the first time in my life found myself on what I have always considered to be the wrong side of the microphone. Word somehow got around and for weeks I found myself touring the country recalling some of my more enjoyable experiences. Now another milestone birthday is looming and I have been asked to bring my notes up to date and tell the inside story of events which people now seem to be eager to recall. And that is what the pages that follow are all about.

Niven's film career started when he got bored with life in the army. Mine began at the age of eight. I was living with my parents in a large country rectory. Today that would probably be taken as a sign of affluence. Then affluence was the last word that came to mind. My father was the vicar of a small country parish. After a distinguished career in the army, which won him a military cross for outstanding bravery, he had finally acknowledged that the injuries he suffered at the battle of Ypres now made it impossible for him to lead the active life he had once enjoyed. His talents were many, but in a small parish they were almost entirely wasted.

On Sundays the church, which has been built to accommodate hundreds of rich Victorians, welcomed a congregation which sometimes swelled to five. The Vicar's Warden always turned up. So did the People's Warden, principally to ensure that no one was able to sit in her pew. As the entire congregation could have arrived in one car, I think she may have over-reacted. I was expected to attend three services every Sunday. It was not something I particularly looked forward to but it did have its compensations. Mrs. Webb (The Vicar's Warden) was rather deaf and used to join in the hymns and prayers about half a verse after everyone else. She would lip read and, when she was sure anyone else who happened to be present was speaking, would join in at a volume which must have put the ancient stained glass windows at considerable risk. Her efforts were supported by Mrs. Green (The Peoples' Warden) who would never be outdone on volume. My father acted as a kind of referee and tried to cope with a situation which would have put anyone else in an early grave. It was country life in the fifties at its best, and an experience I would have been loath to miss.

My mother, who had to cope with running a fourteen room rectory and deal with most of the social affairs of the parish, was the nearest to a saint I shall ever encounter. The family's total income was about £500 a year. Even then it was a derisory sum. On it she had to feed and clothe the family, heat and run the huge rectory, and still adopt a frame of mind which made it seem as if the Christian life she had chosen to adopt was as full of joy as the scriptures proclaimed. It was an impossible task but one which she managed to do with ability and charm. Visiting sick parishioners was one of the duties she felt she should perform. On most occasions that meant going to see people who the rest of the world preferred to forget and attempting to make them feel that somebody cared. It was a gesture which was not always appreciated and one which occasionally produced unexpected results.

Mirabelle Clifton lived alone in a large house at the top of a hill. Her overgrown garden backed on to the local aerodrome. During the war Ms Clifton had caused a stir by complaining that the RAF pilots were circling round her house every night watching her undress. They were actually flying off to Germany but nothing anyone could say would persuade Mirabelle and her well-publicised complaints amused everyone for months. When the war ended she boarded up her windows and became a recluse. From time to time she opened the front door wide enough for food to be passed through, but otherwise she made no contact with the outside world. My mother became concerned about her health and decided that we ought to pay her a visit. It was a trip I still find quite easy to recall.

We arrived at the isolated house as the sun was setting. The windows were all sealed and notices warning that trespassers would be prosecuted were nailed to the front door. Plucking up courage, my mother knocked loudly. We then stepped back and waited. At first there was no response but then we heard a voice. " Go away! You're not wanted."

"It's only me. Mrs. Burder - the Vicar's wife," my mother replied. For a long time there was silence then, just as we were about to move away, we heard locks being unbolted and a lot of muttering from within. Eventually the door was opened but there seemed to be nobody inside.

"Then a voice from the shadows whispered "Come in and don't dawdle I haven't got all day!"

We did as we were told and immediately the door was slammed and bolted behind us. There was almost no light inside and a very unpleasant smell. As we stood there transfixed Mirabelle emerged from the shadows.

"In there! she said, pointing to a small room at the end of a corridor which was piled high with boxes. As we moved forward she drew back the one remaining curtain and dust flew in all directions. In the centre of the room an upturned crate was the main attraction. A few old car seats stood nearby and, in an ancient fireplace, a kettle was balanced on the remains of a fire.

Two cups and a teapot rested on the crate.

Mirabelle moved from the curtain to a cupboard.

"Tea?" she enquired.

Before we could reply, she opened the cupboard and took out a tin. There was a picture of the King on the top of the lid. It had probably been produced to commemorate the coronation many years before. As my mother tried to make polite conversation, Mirabelle opened the tin and tipped some white powder into the pot. Water was added without another word. As the kettle was returned to the hearth my mother looked at me. Her eyes said it all.

They expressed fear and despair but what could we do? There were no potted plants or things we could try to pour the liquid into. Drawing strength from her unquenchable religious faith, mother picked up a cup. I had visions of being orphaned then and there and wondered if I ought to knock the cup out of her hand, but she would not be deterred. She told me later that she was convinced her last moment had come. Fortunately it had not. The liquid turned out to be bicarbonate of soda!

As we prepared to leave I think we felt the visit had been a success. At least we were still alive, but what did Ms.Clifton feel about what for her must have been quite a special occasion? As she closed the door and started to fasten rows of bolts, she delivered her verdict:
"You have been very kind," she said, "and I am not one to forget an act of kindness. I shall be coming to see you in church."
It was a promise we did not expect her to keep but we were wrong. Two weeks later, the congregation at Evensong swelled to four as Ms. Clifton decided to keep her word. Her arrival was impossible to miss. In an attempt to ward off any evil spirits which might attack her as she walked through the village, she had tied all the saucepans she possessed on a string round her waist. As she arrived at church alone, the precaution appeared to have worked,
My father managed to cope with all this surprisingly well. His christian beliefs spurred him through a series of disasters which others might have found impossible to face. When my five-year-old sister Mary died in hospital while being treated for a simple ear infection after a bout of whooping cough, he lost a large part of his life.
When my brother George was killed at the age of 21 a few weeks before the end of the war it as a blow from which dad was never really able to recover. George had joined the army when he left school and served with distinction in the Rifle Brigade. In April 1946 he was shot down while leading his men through a village a few miles from Belsen. Like my dad forty years before, he was awarded the Mmilitary Cross but he never lived to see it. For many years I kept the two medals in a place of honour in my London home. They would still be there today if the house had not been burgled and my two most important possessions taken by someone to whom they would probably mean nothing at all except perhaps the hope of some financial reward.

As the war ended dad was left with me, then aged five, constant pain from his own war injuries, and a job which he must have found poor compensation for the first-class honours he had won at Cambridge many years before. He struggled on with courage and determination. We never had a car or a television, which gave me a few problems later on when I applied for a job with the BBC. Dad travelled everywhere on an old bicycle. At nearly twenty stone he was instantly recognisable, which was perhaps just as well for as his sight began to fail he refused to give up.

"I shall ride on the white line in the middle of the road," he declared. "Then they will see me and know what to do." And that is exactly what he did, for many years - a fact which says as much about the volume of traffic on East Anglia's roads at that time as it does about my father's determination to keep going.

It was my mother who was really responsible for my interest in film. When I was seven, she managed to save enough money to give me a hand-turned film projector as a Christmas present. It was a Pathe Ace and it cost about five pounds. I still have it today. Now it is installed in a place of honour in the cinema I have built in the house where I now live. Today we can watch wide screen films with surround sound and enjoy the advances of new technology. As a child I projected a tiny picture on my bedroom wall (which happened to be blue which made everything look rather sinister.) I endlessly showed the one film I possessed - MICKEY THE VIOLINIST –starring Mickey Mouse. Running time five minutes, filmed in glorious black and white! It wasn't much but for me it was a revolution, and the start of an interest which would eventually take over my life.

Before the arrival of the Ace, going to the movies had involved cycling three miles to the nearest town. There were two cinemas to choose from. One, universally known as the fleapit, was a converted dance hall. Very little had been spent on the conversion and even less on maintenance. Part-time projectionists sometimes managed to show the reels in the right order, but getting every shot in focus usually proved an impossible goal. The Hippodrome was much grander. They employed a commissionaire who spent his days cycling round the county putting up posters, and then returned to don his uniform and clip tickets until the last performance ended. I spent a large part of my formative years sitting in row two, watching pink pleated curtains rise on a variety of films.

At the Hippo they did their best to put on a professional performance. Russ Conway records tinkled away as we entered. At the appointed hour, the lights would dim. Every performance began the same way. The music faded and, as the curtains rose, a slide flashed on the screen - It informed us that "this cinema is disinfected daily with San Izal." After that dramatic announcement, the curtains were lowered and the lights came on again. A cartoon, a newsreel and the main feature followed, and then the audience raced to get through the doors before the national anthem was played. And it all only cost a few pence. One shilling and sixpence of real money, with enough left over to buy an ice cream tub or choc bar if I was lucky. It was an idyllic start to life but more Important things were waiting in the wings.

By the time I was eight I had no doubt about where my future ambitions lay. If I could not be a train driver or a doctor, I knew that I must get into the movies. My parents, who did not share my enthusiasm for Errol Flynn or Doris Day had other ambitions and told me that I must put such silly ideas out of my mind and concentrate on getting a good education.

I attended my first school at the age of five. It was a girls' school - a fact which would have been appreciated more at a later stage. It was only a few minutes walk from home and the headmistress agreed to admit five boys for one term on an experimental basis. I was one of the five. I recall arriving on my first day and being introduced to the head teacher - Miss Buckfield. I was terrified and promptly peed all over the floor! I am ashamed to say that is the only event I can still recall. The next school I attended was much more memorable and some of the events, which occurred there, are indelibly engraved on my soul. St. Augustine's was a well-established prep school run by Benedictine monks. It was set up in Ramsgate, where it was linked to a local monastery. When war broke out and fears of a German invasion were at their height, the school moved to East Anglia, taking over a large country house a few miles from where we lived. My father, having heard about the school's excellent academic record, immediately tried to get me a place. As the son of a local Church of England vicar, I was not what they were looking for, but the war had just ended and schools were all in a state of some confusion. I was offered a place as a day-boy, providing I did not attend any religious knowledge classes - a condition I was more than happy to accept.

Looking back on those days, in one way I find it hard to understand how the school was allowed to operate at all. On another level I am deeply grateful for all they taught me. They used methods which would not be tolerated today but they got results and when we left we had much to be grateful for. The staff were a mixed bunch. Some would have been more at home in a music hall. The monk in charge of catering - Brother Lawrence (inevitably known as Friar Tuck) was type cast for the part. He only had one problem. He could not cook. With wartime rationing still in force and a complete lack of knowledge of anything to do with catering, he faced an uphill task, and it showed. His love of boiled liver - Friday's treat - put me off liver for life and the meals he dished up on other days were just as exciting. Lunch was usually eaten in silence while a senior boy

stood in the middle of the room and read out passages from suitable religious books. At the end of the meal we would all stand and a prayer would be said. The headmaster then opened a small black pocket book and called out a list of the names of boys he wanted to see in his study. Being on that list was what we dreaded most. If our names were called we had to queue outside the head's study while the rest of the school filed past as they left the dining room. After an agonising wait we were then called in, usually one at a time but occasionally as a group. The reason for the call was then revealed.
It could be anything from being late for a class to breaking a window or failing to make the necessary grade in a particular subject. We would be told that the school took a dim view of what we had done and we were going to be suitably punished. The Head would then produce a cane from behind his desk, and instruct us to bend over a table at the end of the room. We were then thrashed extremely hard. The marks lasted for weeks. It certainly made us think about what we had done, but I cannot say it made me any more virtuous. The man who did the caning - our illustrious headmaster - had served in the RAF. A portrait of him in full uniform, complete with medal ribbons, stood in his study and we were able to admire it as we bent over. When the war ended he had returned to the religious order he had served before it began. As a boy I found it was difficult to get to know him. He conducted mass in the mornings, taught us latin during the day and caned us as often as he could. We treated him with a fearsome respect and became very good at Latin because it was too painful to do
anything else. It was, he assured us, the basis of all tongues and a language we could live without. I am sure he believed what he said but I cannot think of a single occasion in my life where all the knowledge I then acquired has been any use at all.
For me the highlights of each term for me were always

the film shows which took place in the main assembly hall from time to time. A projector was set up. The boys all sat on top of clothes lockers which lined the walls of the room and staff occupied two rows of chairs imported the classrooms. When the first scene flashed on the screen there was always a deafening cheer which I shall never forget. Then the magic of the movies took over.
MRS MINIVER was the first film I saw. It was quite topical then, telling the story of an English family's survival during the war at home. It was followed two terms later by THE GREAT CARUSO starring Mario Lanza in a performance which gave most of us our first introduction to classical music. The magic of those shows is still with me now. As I write, I can still feel I am part of that audience of seven to twelve-year-olds, escaping from reality with the help of a silver screen and a youthful imagination.
During my last term I had another brush with show business. Every Christmas the boys performed a pantomime. It was usually a traditional story but for some reason which I cannot now recall, I decided to try to persuade the authorities to do something different. Much to my surprise, they liked the idea and promptly gave me the job of organising it. I thus found myself having to write a school play, and produce it on the last day of term. As I was due to leave for good two weeks later, I decided to live dangerously and write a story set in the school itself. For dialogue I used all the staff's pet Catch phrases. For example, matron always used to say "Now hurry along my darlings."
The Head's best-known pronouncement – "I will see you in my study," required no introduction and most of our teachers had equally recognisable tags. By incorporating them in a story and putting them in other people's mouths - so the Head said," Now hurry along my darlings," and matron promised to see us all in her study, I managed to write my first staged play. It was a gamble. I had visions

of being expelled after the first performance.
On the last day of term the headmaster and his staff took their seats in the front row. A curtain, made out of coloured crepe paper was raised with a piece of string and, with me prompting from the wings and sweating with fear, the performance began. Much to my surprise it was in instant success. From the first few lines, gales of laughter filled the room. The staff recognised a parody of themselves and had the grace to enjoy it. The boys loved every minute and by the time the show ended, for the first and probably last time in life, I had become a hero. The headmaster even smiled and promised to play me his record of The Laughing Policeman - the ultimate accolade anyone at that school could ever expect.
When I started to write this book I thought I would try and contact my headmaster again to find out what he had felt about the school at that time. I expected to hear that that he had retired but my researches had a much sadder end. When I eventually retraced his steps I discovered that he had been murdered some years before by an mentally deranged Scot. A sad end for a man who did a lot of good in his day.
When I left St Augustine's my future course was unclear. I had done well enough to get good exam passes, and my father was keen to continue my education by sending me to a well-known public school. Unfortunately his Church of England stipend just about covered the cost of running the vast rectory I had been brought up in. The prospect of finding thousands of pounds a year to meet even higher school fees was out of the question. The old established public school which he had in mind offered a scholarship and what they felt were generous financial terms but the figures still did not add up so we had to look for other goals. It was then that we heard about Milton Abbey.
Today Milton Abbey is one of the most sought-after public schools in the country. It has an enviable record

of successes. Then it was completely new. We first heard about if from a friend who many years before had been to Clifton College with my father. Unlike dad, he was very wealthy, having been fortunate enough to inherit a large sum of money at an early age. Dad took me to meet him at his flat in Bournemouth. Quite unfairly, I took an instant dislike to him. He was in his seventies and wore an appalling wig which looked as if a very old cat was balancing on his head. His voice was high-pitched and squeaky and the dark clerical suit he wore seemed several sizes too large. We had nothing in common and I was too young and inexperienced to realise where his real qualities lay. Many years later I discovered that he had spent thousands of pounds doing good works, and also paid for me to go to Milton Abbey. It was a very generous gesture, which for years I failed to appreciate or even acknowledge. I fear I was very rude and he must have been very discouraged, though he was far too polite to make any comment. Dad and he were friends and that was all he required. With no input from me, my future for the next five years was decided. I would go to this new English public school and father's friend would pay. It was a decision I would certainly have opposed if I had had a chance. Fortunately that opportunity never arose for the arrangement they reached was to change my life forever.

There are some people who feel it is a good idea to be in at the start of any new venture.

"You are in with a chance of doing something big," my father explained as we arrived to inspect the school which was to be my new home. It was eight miles from anywhere, in the middle of the Dorset countryside. We had seen a prospectus a few days before. It showed pictures of the buildings - once a fine stately home - and spoke in glowing terms about the aims of "The Eton of the West. Britain's foremost educational establishment with new ideas and a progressive future." Dad has appreciated the references to high academic standards. I had been equally captivated by the description of a tuck shop with a soda fountain.

The prospectus painted a very attractive picture, and we arrived with high hopes. We soon discovered that it could have been a contender for the Booker prize for fiction The school it proclaimed and the reality we faced were as different as anyone could imagine. One fact, which the prospectus forgot to mention, was that the school did not actually exist when the glowing words were written. The name had been registered as a school, but it had not yet opened. We arrived to find a vast building which had been used as a faith-healing centre until the operating company's bankers had run out of faith. Since then it had been unloved and empty. We walked around and were beginning to wonder if we had come to the wrong place, when a side door opened and the school's Founder came out to greet us.

The Rev Dr C.K.Francis- Brown, MA, D.Phil. D.Lit. always dressed in black. As he had brilliant white hair, which stood on end revealing a wide and shiny forehead, meeting him face to face could be quite a shock especially at night. He was short and rather pompous - a difficult man to get on with, but one with a number of useful talents. Fortunately he had a large, and charming wife, who smoothed ruffled feathers with ease after years of practice.

Dr Brown had many points to his credit. He had already started and run a successful prep school in Surrey and had recently decided that it was time to move on and establish what he was sure was destined to be the ultimate public school. His main problem was that he did not have any money. Ideas galore, but not much cash, and that can be a problem in any walk of life. In the months before we met, he had managed to persuade a number of backers to provide enough working capital to get the school underway. He had also published the prospectus which he was confident would get things off to a flying start. The first term was due to begin three weeks after we first met. There would initially be twenty-five boys and the total would be increased to two hundred over the first twelve months. I was destined to be one of the first twenty-five.

As we did not have a car, I was instructed to join the school train. At Waterloo I looked for it in vain and eventually discovered that meant joining the last coach of a steam train destined to travel to Blandford Forum - a sleepy town eight miles from the beautiful Dorset village where the school is located.

A letter sent to parents instructed us to then proceed to the Kings Arms public house where were told we should wait outside for the school coach, The word "outside" had been underlined several times so there we stood. Eventually a young man arrived in one smallest cars I had ever seen. It was a 1937 Austin7 designed to carry three. As six boys struggled to climb aboard the young man introduced himself as Bruce Colman who had just been appointed as housemaster of Hambro House.

After a memorable drive we eventually arrived at Milton Abbey. It was the first time I had been away from home and I did not know anyone. We were escorted to a large room which had a table tennis table in the middle and chairs round the walls. It was painted white and to us it was like a prison cell. We sat there wondering what would happen next. Eventually the school chaplain arrived. He was fully robed and had been imported from Dr Brown's prep school as a temporary measure until a full time appointment could be made. He took one look at us and raised his eyes to the heavens.

"Dear Lord" he said quickly adding with an air of desperation in his voice "Please help us", which to me as a thirteen year old boy seemed singularly appropriate at the time. It was the first and the last time we saw him. He left us for ever the following day.

The first twenty-four hours were pretty hellish, but then we began to settle down and a pattern of life emerged. I started to learn Spanish from a textbook written by someone who I am sure must have ended up in a home for the mentally unbalanced. It was all about the life of a pair of complete misfits - Pablo and Rosita -who seemed to move from one totally unbelievable situation to another, using words one would never use in normal life. One example I particularly recall, when translated into English meant -"There is an egg in the middle of the street." I have worked in Spain many times since I left school but have not yet had an opportunity to use that, or most of the other phrases I learned from that memorable book.
We struggled on and the school began to grow. Twenty-five more boys arrived for the second term and made us feel very well established. A few weeks later, when I was quietly walking through the grounds, a bright red sports car skidded to a halt beside me. It looked as out of place as a gorilla at a banquet
"Where can I find your headmaster?" the driver enquired. I told him where I thought Dr Brown would probably be lurking. He then asked my name and thanked me adding words which should have warned my of the dramatic changes that lay ahead.
"I will be seeing you again. I'm your new headmaster."
The car roared away, ignoring the twenty-mile-an hour speed limit and I went back to my daily routine wondering what my afternoon's encounter was all about. That night the news I had been given was officially confirmed. The whole school was assembled and told that Dr Brown was leaving and a distinguished naval officer would be taking his place at the start of the next term. Dr Brown went on to start several more schools. The first - Cokethorpe Park- is today a considerable success. The second did not do well and it is sad to report that at that stage Dr Brown found life such a struggle that he lost

the will to go on and took his own life. His death certificate states that he died of carbon monoxide poisoning. It was a sad waste of a man with many talents and I prefer to remember him for his many successes. With Dr Brown's departure things at Milton Abbey changed overnight. Our new headmaster - Commander Hugh Hodgkinson, DSO. RN. was very down to earth and undoubtedly the right man in the right place at the right time. Having commanded a ship at Dunkirk he knew what being in charge at a difficult time was all about. His presence inspired confidence. Much needed funds began to arrive and a coherent policy for future development started to emerge.

At the time I must confess I was not particularly impressed. One of his first moves was to change the school uniform. Out went gray suits and straw boaters and in came lovat green shorts and pullovers. Not the best way to win the hearts of boys aged 13 and upwards! His second pronouncement - that each day would start with a two mile run, followed by a compulsory cold shower did not go down well either. In retrospect it was perhaps one of the reasons why I have been able to enjoy good health for so many years. As his regime became established the school expanded and grew in importance with the successes it enjoyed. By the time he retired, many years after my departure, Milton Abbey was universally recognised as a good place to be.

At the start of the school's second year of existence there was a major disaster which could have ended the whole project at a very early stage. In January 1956, towards the end of the school's Christmas holiday, the headmaster and his family, who were alone in the school at the time, suddenly smelled smoke. They went to investigate and found the east wing of the building was on fire. Subsequent enquiries established that a workman who was working on the top floor had felt cold and lit a fire in an fireplace which had not been used for years. In a very short time the building was ablaze. Headmaster Hodgkinson, who discovered the blaze, told me later that at the time he was convinced it was the end of Milton Abbey. The first three fire extinguishers he found failed to work so he raced to find a phone and call the fire brigade. The nearest appliance had to come from Blandford, eight miles away, By the time it arrived half of the west wing was ablaze. In retrospect the firemen did a magnificent job. The west wing was destroyed but adjoining areas which, included the magnificent abbots hall and many other rooms with irreplaceable historic features, remained undamaged.

At the end of the term before the fire occurred I had been made a house captain. As one of the senior boys I was invited by the headmaster to return to the school immediately after the fire and help staff to prepare for the new spring term. I vividly recall inspecting the ruins and trying to escape from the smell of smoke which lingered everywhere for months.

Looking back today it is clear that in the long term the fire was not the disaster many had predicted at the time. In some ways it proved to be a great help. The west wing was the least used part of the building. It had not been renovated and the cost of converting it to present day standards would have been extremely high. After the fire the shell was retained and the interior rebuilt.

Clever architects managed to provide four floors where there had originally been three without altering the external appearance of the building. The rebuilding work took nearly two years and while to went on the school continued to grow and make progress.

As the smell or smoke gradually dispersed school activities returned to normal. From time to time normal classes were enlivened by visiting lecturers who spoke with varying abilities on a wide range of different subjects. Most were pretty dire. If attending lectures had not been compulsory I doubt if there would have been anyone to listen to them.

Amid the disasters there were some successes. One of the most popular speakers was Father Potter of Peckham - a Franciscan Friar. He was a down to earth man with a great sense of humour and an extensive knowledge of the life in east London's criminal underworld. His subject was prisons and the people who ended up there and his talks were the only ones for which it was always difficult to get a seat.

Other lecturers sometimes proved to be entertaining for all the wrong reasons. I recall an aged admiral who spent two hours talking about the battle of Matapan. None of us had ever heard of Matapan and did not have the slightest interest in the naval battle which had apparently been fought there but the admiral who delivered the talk quickly became a hit. He had reached an age where it had obviously become difficult to Remember names and facts. He had also devised a complicated diagram to illustrate the progress of hostilities. It involved sticking cardboard ships on a large sheet of blue cloth which was suspended from an easel several feet high. From the outset, much to our delight, everything went wrong. The admiral got flustered and I am ashamed to report that his efforts were greeted with considerable mirth. In spite our lecturer's inabilities I think we all ended up learning something. I learned how painful it can be to stifle laughter for nearly two hours. For some reason the admiral was not asked to address us again.

Another memorable speaker was an elegant middle aged lady who had spent her life collecting old musical instruments. Over the years she had amassed a huge collection which must have been worth a lot Unfortunately her abilities as a public speaker were distinctly limited. Her voice was flat and the clothes she wore made her look as is she herself was a museum exhibit. It was clearly going to be a challenge to establish a rapport with an audience of two hundred teenage boys.

She spent ages laying out her instruments in a long line as we all sat and waited. Time passed and our expectations grew. We all assumed that our guest speaker was about to give an outstanding performance on each of the instruments she had spent her life collecting.

At last the big moment arrived. In a hushed silence our visitor walked to the end of the line and picked up the first instrument which happened to be a flute. We waited and waited and then she blew one note. The flute was put down and the same performance was then repeated with each of the items she had spent so many years collecting and a quarter of an hour laying out. She never blew more than one note and then brought proceedings to an end by saying "Thank you for listening" and walking off. Now I cannot even recall her name but I can remember being in great pain desperately trying not to laugh out loud as the proceedings become more and more of a farce.

Today the are some who question the value of a boarding school education. They feel it is wrong for children to be away from their parents at such a sensitive age. Organised sports are frowned on and often eliminated on the excuse of cutting costs. In the state sector, farcical health and safety laws and reams of petty regulations have put an end to school expeditions and other valuable outside activities. As a result many children are missing out.

When I went back to Milton Abbey for the school's 50th birthday celebrations, I spent a lot of time listening to the boys and girls who are studying there today. I also met many of the staff. They have devoted their lives to providing an all round education which my own experience suggests is an excellent preparation for later life. Passing exams is all very well. For some it will always be the prime goal, but in any worthwhile education academic studies need to be seen in the context of a fuller life. Learning how to live with other people and acquiring as many other skills as possible is more important today than it has ever been. The records of the many who have left Milton Abbey and become successes in the outside world speaks for itself.

When I left school I only had one goal in mind. As the end of my first year at Milton Abbey one of the masters had let me use his clockwork movie camera. It must have been worth about ten pounds but it transformed my life. I used it to document the progress of the school and made what because a major event every term - the school film. I learned far more doing that than I did in the classroom and read books on film and television whenever I could. When the time came to sit my final exams I did not really care. The expected passes were welcome but my interests lay elsewhere. I was determined to get into film and make that my career. As many others have subsequently discovered, that can be a difficult move to make. In those days school careers masters used to recommend the church, the army and insurance and the best prospects for profitable careers. At Milton Abbey they were more adventurous and, as a result many boys went on to do things which they managed to enjoy and to have very successful careers. When I was there as a boy contacts in the film business were hard to come by. With no money coming in, and a father who was about to retire and try to live on a parson's pension, I knew I had to find a job and to get one quickly. A career in film or television was my ultimate goal but in the meantime I realised that I would have to do something else to pay the bills. The question was, what? Without a degree and with no experience of anything, it was difficult to know. It was one of the masters who gave me the idea which eventually got me my first paid job.

As we said our farewells at the end of my last term, he asked where my immediate future lay.

"I haven't the faintest idea," I told him.

"You could always try teaching," he added with a grin. "That's what I did, and look where it has got me!"

He laughed, modestly ignoring the brilliance we had all benefited from. I did not have his brain or anything like it but wondered if his suggestion might perhaps provide me with a temporary income?

I decided to find out more and splashed out some of my last remaining cash on a copy of *The Times Educational Supplement*. It always contained several pages of schools looking for teachers. Most only required those who were well qualified, but on rare occasions it was sometimes possible to find a school which had left it too late to advertise for the experts they really required. As I scanned the pages of the copy I had bought I hoped this would be one of those occasions and so it proved to be.

"Temporary Teacher required for one term at recently established boys school. Ability to teach languages to GCE level and help with day to day running of school. Interest in games an advantage… Apply…."

The advertisement included the name and address of a scholastic agency with a telephone number which I decided to call. Two weeks later I found myself attending an interview with a lady who spoke and looked like Miss Prism in *THE IMPORTANCE OF BEING EARNEST*. Her hair was tied in a bun and her clothes appeared to have been rescued from a period film set. She spent a while studying the papers on her desk then turned to me and asked
" When can you start?"

I explained that I was free immediately. Before I could say more, she gave me a form to sign and then handed me a prospectus for a school which I was now apparently expected to join in two weeks' time. I was surprised and delighted but I was also concerned. I had never been for a job interview before and this was not what I expected. It occurred to me that perhaps Miss Prism thought I was someone else?

I felt I must at least point out that I had no qualifications or experience and was really just filling in time.
" I haven't done anything like this before," I managed to mumble before she cut me off.
" If you're no good we'll soon hear about it. You are the third person we have supplied for this post in the last three months."
She handed me an envelope and then added –
"Everything you need is in here. If there is anything you can't understand, give me a call. The Principal is a Mr. Glynn Davies. He's Welsh" she added helpfully.
Two weeks later I found out what it was all about. The school was a minor independent establishment, run on a shoestring budget and filled with boys who had been unable to pass enough exams to go anywhere else. There were a lot of students from overseas, including two who were French and one Spaniard. As I was due to teach French and Spanish throughout the school, and had only just passed

 GCE exams in those subjects myself, it was clear that I faced an uphill task. Fortunately the boys were co-operative and we managed to get along.
I thoroughly enjoyed teaching. The money was appalling but other rewards were there. There is something very satisfying about being able to encourage young people to do things they have never done before. My problem was that my own knowledge was so poor I had to spend most of my nights reading up the subjects I was due to teach the following day. Somehow it worked and the end of my one-term appointment came very quickly.
For a final treat I decided to take my most senior class to the Shakespeare Memorial Theatre at Stratford-on-Avon. I shall remember that trip for the rest of my days for it was one of those occasions when everything went wrong. I chartered a coach to take the boys from the school to the theatre. With the boys all aboard the coach set of. For some reason which I cannot now recall I

decided to accompany it riding alongside on the on a motorbike that I had recently acquired. That proved to be a big mistake. The bike was very old. It was the only one I could afford. For the technically minded it was a 1947 Francis Barnett 98cc auto-cycle, with rubber front springs and a back pedal brake. At school it had been the butt of many unkind jokes and that night was to provide fuel for many more.

We set off on time, with me riding confidently alongside. it started to rain as we moved away. I had forgotten that it was November the fifth. As we passed through various towns and villages on route I proved to be an easy target and countless fireworks were thrown at me as I tried to keep pace with the school bus on my dilapidated bike. The boys loved it all and encouraging comments poured from the coach. "Go on, sir. Keep peddling! We've got all night."

We eventually arrive at Stratford. A we approached the theatre I noticed that the boys' encouraging comments were being augmented by the voices of people in the town.

"It's Old Mother Riley," someone shouted and another encouraged me to "stop and change the flint!" With the entrance to the extremely smart Memorial Theatre in sight, the final disaster then occurred. My back pedal brake refused to work. I found myself heading for the theatre, at a frightening speed, with no way of stopping. Ticket holders dressed in the smartest clothes, were climbing up the steps. My students were close behind, and there was I, like a drowned rat, heading for the steps at 30 miles an hour. With all the dignity I could muster, I turned the handlebars round and headed for a wall. Bike and wall collided. My front wheel bucked and progress forward stopped. I slunk into the theatre ten minutes later and wished I was not there. The performance of *TWELFTH NIGHT* was very good indeed but for my students it was an anti climax. They had enjoyed my misfortunes far more than any entertainment the Shakespeare Theatre could provide. Riding back, with a buckled front wheel, was another challenge and one which proved to be the highlight of the night.

I left that school at the end of my appointment with about enough money to buy a loaf of bread. I had enjoyed the experience and had probably learned more from the boys I had taught than they had learned from me but my real ambition was still to get into film. It was even more difficult to do that then than it is today. The film industry was completely controlled by unions and television was in its infancy. BBC Television was the envy of the world and the only television channel in the UK. Commercially sponsored broadcasts had not yet started, so opportunities for employment were very limited.

I decided to move to London. With little money saved I needed to get a job and find somewhere to live. As the name of Ealing Studios had appeared on many films I had admired, I decided to try to find a job in that area. The local newspaper contained lists of flats and bed-sits, mostly at prices I could not afford. After viewing many in which I would not have kept a dog I eventually found myself outside a large detached house in Denbigh Road. Mrs. Hedrick, who owned the property answered the door herself. She was wearing what she always wore in the three years I knew her. A dressing gown and bedroom slippers, edged with fluffy pink fur. At three o'clock in the afternoon, on one of Ealing's smarter roads it was not what one expected but Mrs.H. was unperturbed.

"I've come about the bed-sit," I explained.

Mrs. H retreated inside and invited me to follow. The hall was small and painted red and the walls were littered with stuffed birds and stags' heads.

" My late husband," Mrs. H said, indicating the collection. I wondered which one she meant.

We moved upstairs.

"This is it," she announced, opening the door to a room

slightly larger than a cupboard.

"It yours if you want it, and it's all in. Heat, light and washing. You'll get breakfast every morning but I am not partial to preparing meals at all hours so that's all that's it." The room was clean. It was also cheap and I knew it was also the best I could hope for. I paid for two weeks in advance and moved in that night.

Mrs. H proved to be a good friend. When her husband had died or moved elsewhere (I never discovered which) she had decided to let out the rooms and supplement her income selling paintings. As her idea of art seemed to involve splodging oceans of bright colour on canvas, and putting it in a wildly unsuitable frame, most of her money came from letting out rooms and the basement quickly filled with paintings which had proved difficult to sell. Her artistic flair did not amount to much, but her honesty and genuine concern for her tenants' welfare was quite touching. There were three other people living in the building. In the largest room in the house, an unmarried lady in her fifties struggled each night with a one-ring cooker to create what she always described as her "culinary delicacies." She had ambitious ideas but her staple diet was baked beans. She had worked in the hosiery department of a large Victorian department store almost since it was built and her loyalty to the company was very touching. I often wonder what happened to her when the store closed a few years after I had left. I only hope her hard work and loyalty was suitably rewarded. On the floor above there were two other tenants. One worked as the general manager of a local car dealer's showroom. It was a smart place - The Main Dealer for west London he would constantly remind us. He worked hard but his real interest was not in cars. He was a fine musician and for years he had trained to be a concert pianist. When he was unable to find work as a musician he started selling cars so he could earn enough money to be able to eat. Once a year he supervised the production of a musical staged by a local amateur group. I attended one of their performances. They were "doing" *White Horse Inn*. To anyone but the relatives of those who were taking part it was a complete disaster from the moment the curtain went up. The show opened with a big production number. In a Broadway production it must have been terrific but in the hands of an amateur group in a London suburb the impact was not quite the same. Middle aged men in lederhosen pranced about the stage, while ladies of a certain age sang a happy song and milked cardboard cut-out cows with balloons on strings for udders. The cows were fixed to the stage with a few hooks. Unfortunately in the middle of one of the more energetic passages someone pulled the teats too hard. The animals collapsed on the un-swept stage, stirring up clouds of dust which quickly spread far and wide. The cast struggled on but as dust enveloped them their cheerful words we lost in a chorus of coughs and Splutters. It was an unfortunate start and it set the tone for the rest of the evening, which was about as far from perfection any show can be.

Immediately above me in my Denbigh Road broom cupboard, there lived a man we never saw. "Mr. Tom," as he was always referred to by the other residents, was retired and never went anywhere. I never discovered what he had done earlier in life. All I can tell you, after three years living in the room below him, is that he had a habit of taking his boots off at around 3am and dropping them on the floor from a great height. He was also addicted to *The Archers* and would turn the volume of his radio up as each episode reached its climax.

In the midst of all this excitement I had to find a job. With my ultimate goal in mind I decided to call at Ealing Studios. A uniformed commissionaire guarded the small white building on Ealing green. When I explained my mission, he outlined his, which was to ensure that people like me did not get anywhere. I was told to "write in," which I had already been doing for years without any result.

I was beginning to wonder what would happen next, when the local newspaper printed another advertisement which caught my attention.

The advertisement read:

"*Film Distributor requires temporary staff. No experience necessary.*"

I was on the phone in minutes.

Being a film distributor is not one of he most glamorous jobs in the film industry and the company I eventually joined was more modest than most. It distributed films to ships, schools and prisons and a few individuals who had enough money to own projectors. In those days it was quite big business. Video cassettes had not been invented, so for entertainment everyone either went to the cinema, stayed at home watching predominantly live television or attended film shows at one of the locations which I have just mentioned.

I started work in the booking department. It consisted of one very large room with about twenty young girls taking telephone calls and filling in booking cards. We distributed all the latest films. When titles were first shown in the West End of London, sixteen millimetre copies were made for use on ships at sea. Twelve months later they were released to other users so we were kept quite busy trying to allocate copies of each film to the many customers on the company's books. Today that market no longer exists, but then it made money for a few big film companies who provided very little and profited considerably.

Having enjoyed films at school, I was interested to see what happened behind the scenes. On my first morning at work I had the chance to meet one of the people who at school had been a hero - the manager responsible for supplying films to many schools, including my own. I had spoken to him on the telephone a number of times

from the age of fourteen upwards, never thinking I might one day be employed by the same company as he. The meeting shattered all my youthful illusions. He was good at his job but it lacked even the slightest hint of glamour. The highlight of his day was enjoying the vast corned beef sandwiches his wife cut for him each morning. The schools department's activities involved answering phone calls, logging dates on charts and trying to ensure the right film was eventually dispatched to each customer. It was interesting for a day and deadly boring after that. The longest serving employee - I will call her Miss Bond - had worked there for years. To my youthful eyes she seemed as ancient as the first silent movies. In a previous incarnation she had been a civil servant and she ruled the department with a rod of iron. She had what she always referred to as her systems and woe betide anyone who tried to do things any other way. She was not the easiest person to work alongside. With an age difference of at least forty years we had nothing in common but she certainly got results and the success of the business owed a lot to her hard work and grim determination.
I knew my days in distribution were numbered because I quickly got bored. The managers, who were quick to spot my impatience and seemed keen to keep me, moved me around to give me experience of all the different aspects of the business. Unfortunately there were not many aspects to explore. When a grieving mother called to ask us to recommend a film to show to her children while she attended their father's funeral and I recommended *MORNING DEPARTURE*, I began think that perhaps it was time to move on. Once again it was a newspaper that pointed me in the right direction.
The Daily Telegraph had recently carried an advertisement for technical trainees for BBC television. They were looking for people to train as cameramen, sound recordists and editors in the film department, which had recently taken over Ealing Studios. I wrote asking for an

application form and filled it in without delay. Weeks passed and then a letter arrived bearing what for me was then the magic of the BBC logo. Filled with hope I tore open the envelope. The letter was brief and to the point. It thanked me for submitting my application and explained that so many had been received that it would take some time before they were able to make any further response. It was not the encouragement I was looking for. I returned home to help my parents pack up the house and prepare for my father's retirement. At the age of 75, dad had finally decided to call it a day. It was a difficult decision to reach. It meant that the family would soon be homeless and the only money left to live on would be a small church of England pension, and the even smaller amount the army still paid him for his services in the first world war. The beautiful rectory, in which I had been born, was finally cleared, and scraping together every penny they possessed, mum and dad moved to a small mid-terraced property in Brighton. Mum was jubilant. After forty years of cleaning and caring for sixteen rooms, three acres of garden and two lots of stables, she had a tiny house which was easy to manage. Dad was lost without the house he had lived in for so long and the memories that went with it.
As my father's last days of work approached I asked if there was anything he would like to do to commemorate his retirement. He paused to think and then announced "I would like to go to Westminster Abbey."
I started to make the necessary arrangements. As we did not have a car, taxis and trains had to be booked to make the journey. With father leaning heavily a pair of metal crutches we eventually set off and arrived at the main entrance to the abbey. We were not alone. Half the world seemed to have made the same journey and, as we moved inside there seemed to be hordes of people at every point. The Abbey authorities had recently become concerned that their church, which they regarded simply

as a place of worship, was becoming more like a railway station than a place of worship. In an attempt to rectify the situation at intervals throughout the day one of the clergy would climb into the pulpit and make an announcement over
the public address system.
"Will you please now be still and remain silent for a moment so we can remember that we are gathered together in the house of God."
The response was immediate. Wherever they were, people stopped in their tracks and silence returned. Everyone paused - except my father, whose slight deafness had prevented him from hearing the announcement. In an oasis of calm he clattered on, with the metal crutches clanking loudly. When he was about fifty yards ahead of me, he stopped and turned. In a thunderous voice, which echoed round the abbey for what seemed like a hundred years
he announced:
"I must have a pee!" It was a performance he never lived to equal.
Shortly after Dad's retirement, I received another letter from the BBC. It told me that my name had been shortlisted and instructed me to attend for an interview at an address opposite Broadcasting House in London. I arrived in my best suit, with the soup stains cleaned off, for what I felt would be a very special occasion. The waiting room was full and a security man told me that interviews had Already been going on for three days. I sat and waited, wondering what would happen next. Friends had warned me that the going could be tough.
"Note which way the door handle turns when you go in," someone had advised. "It's a catch question to see if you're on the ball." When my name was called, I noted that the handle turned clockwise and went into face a panel of four. The chairman of the appointments board was from what the BBC called the "establishment department"

- a kind of civil service administrative group which appeared to have little to do with programme making. On his right there was a technical manager from the film department, which I hoped to join. Two others with programme production experience, doodled on notepads on the sidelines. After preliminary introductions, the questioning began. The chairman spoke first.
"Perhaps you can start by telling us why you want to join the BBC?" I muttered some tactful remark about wanting to part of the world's best television company and he beamed from ear to ear.
"Good. That's very good," he mumbled, "but it's also wrong. We are not a company. We are a corporation."
I feared I had got off to a bad start. As time passed the atmosphere got less formal. We discussed a wide range of subjects from the newspaper headlines of the day to surviving in London without any money. I told them about the school films I had made and they laughed when I explained how amateur they were. Twenty minutes passed very quickly and I left quite convinced that I stood no hope at all of getting a job. I later discovered that over two thousand people had applied for the six posts which were available. Much to my surprise I was offered one of them and told to report in three weeks time to Ealing Studios.

2 - INSIDE THE BBC

In those happy days the BBC was run by the people who actually made programmes. Management consultants did not exist and accountants were only heard when their advice was actually required. Political correctness, focus groups and critical path analysis were still years away. Everyone was principally interested in making good programmes. The BBC lead the world and it was a great time to be there.

Over the years the BBC had assembled a permanent staff of technicians whose skills were universally recognised as the best in the business. If you kept your mouth shut and your eyes and ears open, it was a great place to learn. After a few brief introductory classroom sessions on red hot subjects like filling in time sheets and the procedures to follow in the event of a nuclear attack, most of our training was done "on the job." In practice that meant that every week we were attached to different production team until we had worked our way round the whole range of the BBC's television programmes. Some attachments were more interesting that others but wherever we ended up it there was always something to learn. I started by working on children's programmes. On my first day in a film cutting room the editor in charge, recognising another pair of hands but failing to appreciate how inexperienced they were, put me to work the moment I arrived.

"It's *Andy Pandy* this week," he announced. "The big reel over there is today's programme. The two smaller ones are titles. I want you to find the right title for today. When you have got it, join it on and take it up to telecine. And watch out!" he warned. "The titles aren't all the same. One says Andy Pandy is in his little house today. Let's go join him . The other says he's in his bleeding garden. If you use the wrong one we'll get hundreds of letters from miserable kids. So watch it! When

you've finished you'll find me in the bar."
With that he was gone, and I started my professional career.
After an exhilarating week on Andy Pandy I was promoted to *The Flowerpot Men*. It was not exactly life in the fast lane, but it was all good experience. I was then posted to the BBC's most prestigious arts programme - *Monitor*. I was not the only new arrival. A trainee producer had just been employed. He was a young man who had already made a superb documentary about a block of flats in which he had once lived. As he never tied his shoelaces and worked extremely long hours I wondered how long he would survive. His talent was so great and his personality so charming I need not have worried. His first BBC programme was a documentary on the life of the Russian composer Prokofiev. He quickly moved on to bigger things. His name was Ken Russell.
When you have no professional experience of film making, a cutting room is an excellent place to start to acquire the knowledge you need if you are going to make anything worth watching. Editing in one of the most important jobs in film and television. To an outsider, an editor's work simply involves cutting out the bad bits and assembling scenes in the right order. The reality is more complex. A good editor can make a programme which has been filmed adequately but without any particular flair more interesting to watch. To do that he must have the right materials to work with. He will need shots filmed from several different angles. They must be shot in a way which will enable them to be cut together satisfactorily. If they have been filmed from the wrong positions, or if continuity considerations are ignored, when they are assembled in the cutting room the action will be unnatural and it will appear to jump. For example, if a director shoots two shots showing someone getting out of a car and putting money in a parking meter, he (or she) needs to ensure that the action

overlaps and corresponds at the planned cutting point. He could start with a general view, showing the whole car coming to a halt and the driver getting out. He might then decide to film another shot simply showing the driver in close up. In the cutting room, it should be easy to cut the two shots together, providing the basic rules of continuity have been observed. If they have been overlooked, and the driver is looking straight ahead in the long shot and to the right in the close-up, when the two scenes are joined the action will appear to jump and the effect will be disturbing. Working in cutting rooms you start by learning basic lessons like that which are an important part of making any professional film.

Working with Ken and a very experienced editing team, I managed to learn a lot of lessons it would have taken much longer to master in other hands. It was great fun and every week we turned out a different thirty minute programme, all largely shot on film with a minimum of live studio inserts.

I was just beginning to feel I might eventually be able to make a useful contribution to the *Monitor* team's efforts, when I was told that I would be moving to sport. It was not news I wanted to hear. At school, while others waited eagerly for rugby matches to start, I had prayed for rain, in the hope that we might be sent on a cross-country run and escape from captivity for a couple of hours. Sport has never interested me but it does form a very large part of television output.

When I joined the BBC in the 1960s most programmes, including sporting events, were transmitted live. They were seen as they happened. If mistakes were made the viewers were able to enjoy them too. With a sports like cricket, which some Englishmen seem to regard as religion, that made life tough for our team of commentators, whose every word was weighed up by a host of armchair critics. If one word was mispronounced or uttered in a way which was not totally conventional, irate

viewers would pick up their phones and call the BBC, to protest about what they felt was a disgraceful use of the English language. If a programme was ever taken off the air o interrupted at any point which viewers felt disturbed the flow of play, there was hell to pay, so decisions to curtail any advertised programme were usually taken at a fairly senior level. My involvement was at the other end - as one of the most junior members of a production team. When I first joined, videotape had not then been invented but as programmes were transmitted live they
were often recorded simultaneously on film for repeat showing later and for sale to overseas television networks. For test match cricket, every ball of every day's play was recorded on 16mm film with the sound alongside. The recordings were made at Lime Grove Studios in West London. As each thirty-minute reel of film was completed it was taken off the recording machine, unloaded in a photographic darkroom and then given to a motor cycle despatch rider who then took it to a film processing laboratory in north London. Each roll took up to two hours to develop and print a copy. The despatch riders then brought the film back to Lime Grove where teams of editors worked against the clock to produce an edited version for transmission that night. It is not easy cutting six hours' play down to thirty minutes without accidentally missing some important highlight which will instantly encourage cricket enthusiasts to reach for their phones but we did it day after day. The same procedure was followed for Wimbledon tennis and for all the other major sports. As there were no other television channels the BBC showed everything and there were very few complaints.
When I had finished work one night, and was arranging for a courier to take our edited version to Heathrow and put it on an overnight flight to Australia, I met a very senior engineer who happened to be passing. "You won't be doing that much longer," he said. " Film

has had its day." Over a couple of beers in the BBC club, he told me that he was part of a team which had been working on a new method of recording sound and pictures on magnetic tape. It was code named VERA – I think the letters stood for Vision Electronic Recording Apparatus. A prototype machine was already on test. It was exciting news, for the new machine could apparently play back recordings immediately they were made. There would be no more delays for film processing and tapes could be erased and used again so costs would be dramatically reduced. The machine my colleague described apparently took up most of a room but he had no doubts that it was where the future lay. It sounded like a good idea and I felt that in due course the BBC would make an announcement about its revolutionary new product, but that announcement was never made. The Americans and the Japanese produced far more compact systems, which quickly dominated the market, and the age of the video recorder began.

Today almost everything is recorded either on videotape or on a computer disks. I cannot claim that I have found it makes cricket more exciting to watch but it certainly makes it much easier to edit!

One of the less creative jobs we found ourselves involved in as our training progressed, was the adaptation of American television programmes for British use. The work sometimes had to be done very quickly and it did not always go according to plan. At that time *THE PERRY COMO MUSIC HALL* was a big American hit. It was produced in the USA, where it was screened from coast to coast. A film recording was then put on a plane and sent to London overnight. It arrived at Heathrow in the early hours. After checks by customs officials it was brought to Ealing Studios where we had a few hours to adapt it for UK showing the same night. It was usually a fairly straightforward task. We had to remove the American commercials and any references Perry made to

commercial products in the course of the programme. That was not always as simple as it may sound. In the USA at that time the show was sponsored
by Kraft and Perry would sometimes make glowing References to Kraft's wide range of products as he introduced his songs. I can't recall the exact words he used but it was probably something like."
Now, thanks to our sponsor Kraft- who make those great cheese dips in the easy-open cartons, I'd like to sing you my latest song". ….
For UK audiences comments like that had to be removed. We then had to ensure that our edited 35mm
film copy still looked pristine. I was told that the work normally took a couple of hours but on the day I joined the team responsible for this task, that situation was about to change.
A new high-powered re-winding machine has just been installed. When the necessary cuts had been made, the edited programme was placed on the new equipment to be rewound and cleaned. The reel of film was Exceptionally large. It contained three thousand feet of 35mm film - three times more than a standard UK reel, and consequently three times the weight.
My colleague pressed the start button and the new machine sprung to life. As we stood and watched, it gathered speed. It soon became clear that, with the added weight, it was running too fast. It started to shake and slid across the floor. We stepped back for our own safety and watched as the film shot off the reel and flew out of a window. It landed in a car park two floors below!
In retrospect we should probably have laughed but with only two hours to transmission it was not a situation we could then enjoy. We raced from the cutting room wondering what we would find when we reached the car park. We were lucky. The film had landed on the roof of a car. It was dusty but undamaged. Two hours later it was shown to several million viewers and nothing more was

ever said - until now!

In the course of my training I was involved in a number of other incidents where disasters of one kind or another were averted at the last minute by skill or luck.

One of the prestige highlights of the year was always the Christmas broadcast by Her Majesty the Queen. In those days I seem to remember, it was recorded several weeks before the festive season. Outside broadcast vans were sent to Buckingham Palace and a selection of BBC VIPs (and those who felt they were VIPs but weren't!) descended on the Palace to give Her Majesty what they all thought was helpful advice. The sheer terror that advice produced could be judged from her expression on the screen. Her Majesty should be forgiven if she sometimes looked as if a posse of assassins were standing behind the camera. They were!

In those days the royal broadcast was produced on film for international. Shots of the outside of Buckingham Palace were joined on at the start and end. Copies of the final edited version were then prepared for dispatch to all the world's major television companies. Each copy was accompanied by an official letter, written on Buckingham Palace notepaper and signed by a very senior royal official. It explained that the programme must not be shown anywhere in the world before 9am on Christmas day.

From a film point of view editing that programme was one of the simplest jobs of the year but there was one occasion when it became a nightmare.

A few days before the programme was recorded, an ex-employee had visited the cutting rooms to see the colleagues he used to work with. He brought with him an exceptionally blue movie, which he reluctantly agreed to leave for a few days so it could be seen by some people who were working on later shifts. With the royal message in production, the blue movie was temporarily forgotten. When its owner returned a week later, to everyone's dismay the copy he had left with us could not be found. We tore the place apart and looked everywhere. As time passed a really dreadful possibility began to dawn. Perhaps someone had put the wrong film in the wrong can? If it had happened, we knew that somewhere in the world there must be a film can containing a very blue movie accompanied by a sealed letter from Buckingham Palace. As the letter specified that the film must not be shown until Christmas day, it seemed that someone somewhere could be heading for a shock. The possibilities were too awful to discuss. No one knew what should be done. For days we sweated and prayed then, just as a full confession was about to be made, the missing film turned up. A technician from another department had borrowed it and failed to tell anyone what he had done!

As my training continued I found myself working for short periods on a wide variety of programmes with many of the biggest names of the day. For a country boy, who had been taught at school to call everyone older than me "sir" being on first name terms with people whose fame had made them household names took a lot of getting used to. As a national television network the BBC has to transmit many hours of programmes every week. Some are designed to appeal to the widest possible audience. Others are aimed at minorities with specialist interests. Today the BBC shows a higher percentage of repeats and imports than it has ever done, as the all-powerful accountants cut costs at every stage and opt for mediocrity. When I was being trained, we took great pride in the shows we produced and had a first-class team of professionals, with many different skills, on the permanent payroll. As a trainee I was expected to spend a few weeks on as many different shows as possible. That meant that one month I might be working on filmed inserts for a major drama series and a few weeks later find myself on *PANORAMA* or one of the other programmes produced by the talks Department. That could be followed by a few weeks on situation comedies like *STEPTOE AND SON* or *DAD'S ARMY*. It was a wonderfully varied life and it gave me the sort of all-round-training, which today no one is able to provide.

The drama department alone produced hundreds of shows every year. They included prestige one-off plays and dramatisations of Dickens novels, transmitted as serials over several weeks. There were series like *DOCTOR FINLAY'S CASEBOOK, and ALL CREATURES GREAT AND SMALL,* all made on the sort of budgets which today might just cover the cost of a basic commercial. All these programmes were transmitted live though they sometimes included pre-filmed inserts. - a tremendous feat when you think how many things could go wrong, and often did.

Programmes like *DR FINLAY'S CASEBOOK* were written by experienced television dramatists who based their stories on characters and situations created by A.J.Cronin and adapted them to meet the needs of a television studio and a fairly restrictive budget. Much of the action took place in the doctor's surgery - Arden House. A set showing the surgery, living room and various other areas was built for the series and assembled each week in one of the larger studios in the new BBC TV centre at Shepherds Bush. Exterior scenes were filmed in advance at Callender in Scotland. Bill Simpson, Barbara Mullen and Andrew Cruickhank starred in what quickly became one of the BBC's most popular drama series. Twenty six programmes were made in the first year (1962) and other series followed later. Early episodes were produced by Julia Smith, one of the most able women in television, who went on to pioneer the first series of *EASTENDERS* which soon developed into the nation's favourite "soap".

Some weeks before the *DR FINLAY* programmes were

transmitted, the cast and a film crew would set out to pre-film sequences at a number of carefully selected locations which were often in Scotland. Scenes which were considered too difficult or too expensive to stage in a studio were shot on 35mm film and sent to us to be edited at Ealing studios. We had scripts for each complete episode and cut the pre-filmed inserts to match those scripts. By the time cast and crew arrived at the locations they had studied the scripts and everyone knew what we wanted to achieve. Everything which could be prepared in advance had been taken care of, but when you are working on location there are still plenty of things which can go wrong. The Great British Public - our viewers (bless them) were the cause of many a retake.

The crew could spend ages preparing to shoot quite a complex scene only to have all their efforts ruined at the last minute by someone doing something they were unable to control. In the middle of a 'take' someone would emerge from a house wearing jeans, which did not fit in with the 1930's atmosphere we are attempting to create. On other occasions jumbo jets would pass overhead or someone would emerge from nowhere, and approach actors the middle of a scene and ask "Are we on telly?"

Dr FINLAY'CASEBOOK was what is known in the business as a period piece and the costumes and sets used for studio scenes were designed to reflect the period the action was set in. When real locations were used for the filmed inserts, the same rules applied and anything modern had to be banished from sight. If you think of the average street or shopping area you will soon realise how difficult that can be. Satellite dishes have to be concealed or removed. Parking meters must be disguised or framed out of shot. Modern windows can be edged with ivy or hidden in some other way and street lights usually require attention. It takes time and requires a wide range of different skills which at that time BBC staff had in abundance.

Sometimes we encountered things which even the most talented designer can find hard to disguise. In one of the films I worked on, we had to shoot scenes outside a very beautiful church. The location was just right for the period we were attempting to recreate. It was in an area where over the years very little had changed, and when street lights had been suitably doctored and roads cleared of modern vehicles it looked much as it would have done on the day when our scene was supposed to be taking place. One obstacle remained. There was a large electrical transformer a few yards from the place where our camera needed to film. It was impossible to shoot from any other angle, so the transformer had to be either hidden or removed. As removal would have meant plunging the whole area in darkness possibly for days, the production designer was asked to come up with a better idea. In a few hours he managed to create what looked like an old war memorial, using plastic and paint. It was duly moved into a place which hid the transformer and filming continued without inconveniencing anyone.

In television today time is money. Fully equipped studios are expensive to run, so much of the preliminary work on any television drama is usually done away from the studio in which the programme will eventually be performed. While location film shots are being edited, the cast will assemble in a rehearsal room to run through the script. Rehearsal rooms can be bleak. There will be a table and chairs and possibly a few key "props" but the most important part of the room is the floor. The points at which there will be walls and furniture when the production moves into a studio will be marked out in chalk so the actors moves can be planned and rehearsed. The cast will use their rehearsal time to get into character in their various roles and to work out where they need to be at each point. A day or so before transmission, they will move into a fully equipped studio. Then, for the first time, they will be working with sets, lights and cameras all around them. The first few hours of studio time is usually be spent arranging lights and positioning cameras. As the day proceeds, outstanding problems are gradually be resolved. There will then be a full camera rehearsal, (often referred to as a final run-through) with everyone in costume. The next performance will probably be the one which audiences will see and in my day that usually meant a live transmission.

If you have not had an opportunity to stand in a Television studio a few minutes before transmission you may not fully appreciate the tension which can be present on such an occasion. I still recall my first experience of live television, from those first few weeks when I was as a trainee. We had been editing the film sequences for a play, which was about to be performed, and had come to the studio to watch the live transmission. It had been a frantic day. Rehearsals had started at eight in the morning. There had been camera breakdowns, an artiste with gastric flu and a number of other off-screen dramas. The final rehearsal had been pretty disastrous, as quite often happens. Actors had missed their cues and consequently come on at the wrong time or in the wrong place. A camera had moved left in stead of right and consequently appeared in shot, looking very out of place in a 17th century drawing room. There had been an increasing air of tension as the day went on and the floor manager's "Well done everybody," at the end of the run through had not convinced anyone.

As the studio doors closed cutting off the set from the outside world, my watch showed that there was one minute to go before we went on air and the live transmission started. We all knew that sixty seconds from now, around ten million people would be watching everything that happened in our studio. The floor manager made the final announcement - "Right studio. Quiet please. We have one minute...."

When you sit at home and watch a television play, I hope it looks real and carries you away, so you feel totally involved in the action of the plot. If we have done our job properly, you will find what you see appears to be completely natural. If we are off form you will quickly spot errors and feel the programme is dull and probably not worth watching. At the end of the day it's professionalism that counts. While you are resting in your armchair, a team of highly trained people is sitting in a small room looking down on the studio where the actions you are watching are taking place. The room Is known as the *gallery* and the scenes being performed In the studio are relayed to it from a number of cameras on the studio floor. The programme Director, a Vision Mixer and other key members of the production team watch the action on rows of monitor screens. Each screen shows the output from one camera. At points planned in the script and indicated by the Director, the Vision Mixer will cut from one camera to another, selecting the shot you will see on your screen at home. If the action involves scenes which have been pre-filmed on location, a videotape machine will be cued in to play those inserts at precisely the right moments. Timing is crucial. If pre-filmed sequences are cued at the wrong point the action talking place in the studio may not match the shots which have been recorded in advance. For example, if an actor walks out of a studio set showing the hall in his house and then gets into a car outside in shots which have been pre-filmed, the timing must be exactly right. If the pre-filmed sequence is cued too soon, the car may drive off before the studio actor gets out of the room. If it is cued too late, he may seem to be in two places at once. Everything must precisely controlled and in a television every second counts. As the action proceeds, the crew in the gallery will follow the action on their scripts. Each page contains a number of shots, with the dialogue to be spoken, the actions performed and the camera responsible for that shot specified alongside. As the Vision Mixer cuts from one camera to another, a production assistant will call – "Scene 27 on 1. Camera 4 next," and so on, to ensure everyone is aware of what is about to happen, and (hopefully) get the right shots in the right order by cutting or mixing from one to another at precisely the right point.

Of course inevitably mistakes are made from time to time. Today errors can be corrected before programmes are shown because most shows are now pre-recorded. In the 1960s trainee mistakes were far more common. Occasionally someone would cut to the wrong camera and audiences would be treated to a glimpse of something they were never meant to see. There were times when actors slammed doors so hard that walls collapsed and there were numerous occasions when equipment, which had worked perfectly in rehearsals, failed to perform when we were live on air.

Caption cards explaining that *NORMAL SERVICES WILL BE RESUMED AS SOON AS POSSIBLE* were then displayed and soothing music was played while we frantically tried to find out what had gone wrong and to solve the problem as quickly as possible. On most occasions, miraculously things did so according to plan, possibly because everyone involved had been trained to a high degree and we all shared the same objectives. There wasn't an analyst or a manager who not been actively involved in production anywhere around.

From the drama department I moved to talks - the group responsible for many of the BBC's most prestige shows which then included *PANORAMA* and a nightly magazine programme called *TONIGHT*. Both were transmitted live from the Lime Grove Studios in Shepherds Bush. *PANORAMA* concentrated on politics and major national issues. Its main presenter then was the legendary Richard Dimbleby. In my humble view, no one has every surpassed his ability and style in handling studio Interviews and making state occasions interesting to watch.

PANORAMA broke new ground by exploring a number of taboo subjects in a much more direct way than anyone had ever dared to attempt before. At that time there were very few television interviewers would have dared to say "boo" to a goose on camera. There was an air of respect for anyone in authority yet Prime Ministers and big names from industry regularly accepted invitations to appear on the PANORAMA. Dimbleby was every inch a broadcasting professional. His huge figure inspired confidence and created an air of authority but his real strength lay in the way he meticulously prepared for everything he agreed to take on. Later in life, he was asked to provide the commentary for a number of live broadcasts of major national events. He often spent weeks researching every detail of the subjects he knew he would have to comment on. On the day of transmission the results of his research would be neatly written on summary cards which he kept before him in case of need. He was the ultimate anchor man and everyone who had the good fortune to work with him learned a lot.

In those days *Panorama* was the ultimate prestige programme. It was transmitted at peak viewing time and was highly respected for its professionalism and for the views it expressed. Shortly after I arrived a few key members of the production team hatched up a plan which they felt would enable them to have a laugh at their audience's expense. No one on had ever dared to do anything like that before and when their idea was first mooted there were a number of senior BBC executives who nearly had a fit. In conditions of great secrecy a specially shot item was prepared for a programme due to be transmitted on April 1st. (April Fools Day in the UK) The items purported to be a live report from Italy where spaghetti production was apparently enjoying an all time

boom. In the report Dimbleby explained how spaghetti bushes were producing hitherto unknown quantities of the highest quality crop. We saw how the spaghetti was harvested by hand from the bushes it had grown on. It was all presented as a down to earth factual report and when it was shown, for a while it caused quite a stir.
As you are no doubt aware, spaghetti does not grow on bushes. The whole story was designed as a hoax for April fools day. Unfortunately, as it was presented as a factual report, with all the seriousness of a normal *Panorama* item, many people believed what they were being told. Within minutes of the start of the programme BBC telephone switchboards were jammed with calls from people all over Britain. Questions were asked in Parliament and enquiries held at senior management level. For a while it seemed as if no one could take a joke but eventually it all calmed down and most people realised it was simply a hoax. It was an interesting experiment and it showed once again that people tend to believe anything they see on television. Of course, as every schoolboy knows, spaghetti actually grows in tins!
PANORAMA was one of the first television programmes to transmit a live outside broadcast from overseas. Today almost every news programme includes live shots from anywhere in the world and even from outer space. An electronic revolution has turned what to us then were dreams into everyday events. The whole pace of life is faster and one can now instantly speak on television to anyone anywhere in colour, with high quality sound, at any time of the day or night.
In the 1960's all television was black and white. By today's standards it was in many ways a pretty amateur affair but at the time BBC television programmes were universally respected as the best in the world. The Corporation set standards which other television networks strove to emulate. Some eventually succeeded by employing many of the BBC's staff and by pioneering

new ideas and techniques which they made their own. The biggest revolution of all has been in technology. Electronics were then a relatively new industry. Cinemas, which relied on films shot on conventional photographic film, were a familiar part of everyday life but the idea of producing pictures and sounds instantly by using Electronics was just beginning to make commercial sense. Exciting opportunities were being revealed and I was fortunate enough to be involved as the new technology first began to take off.

I can still recall how we were transfixed when Richard Dimbleby stood in the harbour in Calais, and spoke live from France to us in England at the start of a *Panorama* programme. It seemed as if a miracle had been achieved for pictures and sound to travel so far. The pictures were of course in black and white and their quality was so poor it looked as it was snowing across the English channel, but it was a live transmission. We were seeing what was happening at that moment and in those days that was a huge event. Now, when broadcasts from all over the world and even the moon are received as they happen, it all seems very tame, but the pictures we saw then were breaking new ground in a way which then only the BBC seemed able to do.

The *TONIGHT* programme, which I joined next also broke new ground. It went out live five days a week, around seven o'clock in the evening, and consisted of live studio interviews and filmed reports with people who the producers thought viewers would find interesting to watch. They managed to strike a balance between keeping people informed on the serious issues of the day and introducing them to a more eccentric side of life. Nowadays television magazine programmes so often feature people who want to promote their latest records, or politicians who are chosen because they can rattle on for hours, and not expect a large fee. In the 1960s the viewers came first. Programmes were not devised on a

basis of how much money could be saved but simply on how entertaining they would be. People with ideas and creative talents were firmly in control. As a trainee I joined the *TONIGHT* production team for a short time. From our point of view the key point
about the programme was that it was topical. It went out live every weekday evening at a time when most people were just getting home from work. That meant a lot of material was needed and it had to be prepared very quickly. Each programme ran for around 30 minutes and consisted of a few studio interviews and a lot of stories which were pre-filmed at locations all over Britain and overseas.
Each show would end with a song from the programme's resident singers - Robin Hall and Jimmy McGregor. With the benevolent Cliff Michelmore anchoring the show, it was good family entertainment and every night millions of people watched.
Behind the scenes on *TONIGHT*, the pace could be frantic. Because it was a topical show, the filmed stories were often shot on the day they were shown. Today that is normal practice. With videotape and live satellite links a story can be captured and presented very quickly. In the 1960s it was far more complex. Every morning the programme's editorial team would meet and make a list of the stories they wanted to cover. Film crews, consisting of a reporter, a film Cameraman, a camera Assistant and a Sound Recordist, would be dispatched to shoot Whatever it was felt was required. While they were away, the Studio Director contacted the people he wanted to come to Lime Grove studios to be interviewed there. Many superb reporters worked on the programme - Fyffe Robertson and Alan Whicker to name just two. Only the best could survive because there was no time for errors. The *TONIGHT* crews travelled far and wide. For example, one day light aircraft crashed into the English Channel. A reporter and film crew was dispatched from London

airport to fly to air sea rescue headquarters in Cornwall. They had to establish the facts, shoot their report at breakneck speed and then get the exposed film back to London. It then had to be processed by an outside Laboratory so we could see what was on they had shot. While the film was being developed, the sound which they had recorded on a quarter inch tape was re-recorded on perforated magnetic film ready so it too could be edited. On a good day unedited rolls of sound and picture would arrive in the cutting rooms around lunchtime but there were often unexpected delays. We sometimes only received the material we had to work with around 4 o'clock in the afternoon. That just left three hours to cut picture and sound and devise, write and record a commentary for what was sometimes quite a long story. And there were many even tighter deadlines. I seem to recall that we stared editing the air sea rescue story I mentioned earlier just as the first item in the programme was going on the air. There were many occasions when the first part a report was being transmitted while commentary for the second reel was still being recorded. As transmissions were made from a tele-cine suite on the ground floor, the cutting rooms were on the 7th floor and the sound dubbing suite on at an intermediate level things got pretty tense at times!

From time to time things did go wrong. A film splice might break and screens go blank. Sound and picture would occasionally slip out of synchronisation, so the sound audiences heard did not match the actions of the people on the screen. When difficulties arose, Cliff would move smoothly into action and purr out excuses and Robin and Jimmy would sing another song while behind the scenes all hell broke loose as we desperately tried to sort out the problem. Fortunately there were very few breakdowns, which says a lot about the quality of the key people who were involved. They were ace technicians who it was a privilege to know. As producer Tony

Essex and senior Editor Alan Tetzner were old hands. Viewers were rarely disappointed by the results of their efforts.

Today I am afraid the people who now control television output would prefer to show yet another cookery or home improvement programme or fill the spot with a games show which is cheap and easy to produce. Now everything is made for the lowest possible price. It has to be cheap and politically correct and, as a result, today's television viewers are missing a lot.

As my training continued we were able to take advantage of a number of new technical developments. All television pictures were still in black and white but low definition 405-line pictures were soon replaced by a higher definition 625-line system. That meant that it looked as if it was snowing rather less often.

Photographic films became more sensitive to light so less power was needed and studios became cooler and less like a sauna. Cameras got smaller and the age of micro-technology began. The first tie-pin-sized radio microphones came into use. For the first time sound could be transmitted by a radio link from a tiny clip-on microphone to a portable receiver held just out of shot. Today this is standard practice. The equipment involved usually works but in the early days it had a number of drawbacks. Recorders were apt to pick up not only the sound you wanted to record, but also anyone else who happened to be using the same wavelength. Interviews with politicians outside parliament would sometimes be enlivened by the down-to-earth comments of any taxi drivers who happened to be passing or by someone ordering fish and chips from a nearby takeaway.

As my three year training course neared its end I found myself being attached to some of the departments I had so far missed. At that time the BBC was a also a world leader in light entertainment. Comedians like Tony Hancock had made the transition from radio to television and his writers - Ray Galton and Alan Simpson had created the ultimate in what became known as situation comedies. For many years Jimmy Perry and David Croft devised, wrote and produced some of the funniest shows ever seen on television. *DAD'S ARMY, ALLO! ALLO!* and *ARE YOU BEING SERVED?* were among their many brilliant creations. They set and maintained very high standards.

If the ideas which proved to be so successful then were submitted for approval to those who responsible for light entertainment today I very much doubt if they would ever be made. In their own way they were all politically quite incorrect. Today there is no one in the BBC who would have the courage or authority to commission programmes like that. There is also no one left with the production experience to instantly realise just how successful they would be.

The shows I have just mentioned worked because they were superbly written and professionally produced. Today the actors and actresses who appeared in them have become household names but when those shows were first made they were mostly unknown to television viewers. Some had considerable experience of acting in the theatre but very little else. The Croft / Perry team and those who were encouraged and trained by working with them, produced cost effective shows which are now generally regarded as all time classics. When DVD copies of television shows are released today, there is a huge demand for shows made over thirty years ago while many more recent productions are instantly forgotten. Audiences know that good shows are not the result of bowing to the demands of management committees. Accountants and systems analysts do not know where to place a camera to make a scene work or how to write a line and deliver it so it gets a laugh. Until the administrative minions are replaced by qualified technicians who know what television production is all

about, current problems will remain unsolved.
When John Birt was the BBC's Director General a Collective pool of resources and talents, which had made BBC Television the envy of the world, was gradually dispersed. There are many who feel that his policies and the management structures he introduced did untold damage and encouraged many of the biggest talents to move out of television.
As a trainee I was able to work with and observe many of the great creative geniuses of the day. I remember walking down to the Riverside studios in Hammersmith to watch Tony Hancock in action. He had been a huge name on radio with *HANCOCK'S HALF HOUR* which became a national institution. When he made the difficult move from radio to television the hugely talented scriptwriters who created his programmes - Ray Galton and Alan Simpson - provided him with more excellent material and his continuing success seemed to be assured. His shows included guest appearances by many other highly talented actors and he was supported by a loyal and talented cast which included Sid James - now best remembered for his work on the *CARRY ON* fims.
Hancock was a difficult man to work with. He was very a very big name but he lacked self confidence and he found it difficult to learn, rehearse and perform a new thirty minute show every week. His shows were transmitted live from the Riverside studios in Hammersmith after a week of rehearsals. As videotape recorders has not yet been invented Hancock's programmes, like many other smash hits of the time, might have been lost and forgotten if the BBC had not been experimenting with new techniques when the shows were made. When they were transmitted live from Hammersmith the output from the studio was simultaneously sent along a telephone line to the Lime Grove studios in Shepherds Bush where it was recorded on film in black and white for archive purposes.

A relatively new department then called BBC Enterprises, had plans to sell copies of the recorded shows to overseas countries but as the quality of the 16mm film recordings was not very good they were not overwhelmed by an instant demand. As a trainee one of my jobs was to edit those recordings which I did in a cutting room on the 7th floor at Lime Grove with *MAIGRET* and *SPORTSVIEW* being edited simultaneously in rooms on either side. Today those recordings have been rescued. Recent developments in technology have enabled them to be digitally enhanced and released on DVD.

There is even talk of using computer technology to prepare colour versions of shows which were first transmitted over forty years ago in black and white.

I have just seen a restored DVD copy of a Hancock programme which I edited on film in 1961. It was one of his biggest BBC successes - *THE BLOOD DONOR*, which was produced by one of the BBC's most talented Producers of comedy shows – Duncan Wood.

Watching the show today brings back vivid memories of the day on which it was made. For Hancock himself the day had got off to an unfortunate start. While driving to the studio to start work his car had been involved in an accident. It wasn't a major crash but it was clear from the moment he arrived that Hancock had been shaken up. We were all concerned that he might be unable to perform. He was never particularly good at learning his lines and the accident had clearly made things worse. Fortunately on that day help was at hand.

If you watch *THE BLOOD DONOR* today (and it is still widely shown) you may notice that while Hancock gives his usual competent performance there are occasions when the lines he delivers are not spoken directly to the people they are intended for. When Hancock is talking to someone you can see the conversation taking place but if you look closely at what is going on you will notice that he is looking slightly above or to the left or right of the person he is addressing. At first site the situation is not that easy to spot When the shows were transmitted live viewers failed to notice anything amiss but in the studio we knew what was going on. When Hancock turned his head casually aside most people thought it was part of his act but we knew he was actually looking for his next line on what is now known in the trade as an idiot board or some other prompting device strategically placed just out of shot.

Today prompters are in general use. They are usually known by the brand name of one particular type which you will find in studios all over the world - Autocue. When Hancock's programmes were performed prompters were new and only used as a last resort. But after *THE BLOOD DONOR* Hancock relied on them for the rest of his career. Using modern equipment is now normal for an actor to appear to be taking directly to the camera lens while his lines are displayed on a screen which audiences cannot see. In Hancock's day his lines were written on boards which were hidden all over the place just out of shot.

Hancock's last BBC series was made in 1961. By then it was obvious that changes would inevitably take place. For years his shows had been written by two of the best writers in the business and he had been supported by a loyal and able cast. But Hancock never like to feel his performance was being eclipsed. Over the years he gradually fell out with most of the people who worked with him. As his confidence failed, a celebratory drink after the show became a bottle a day and it went on from there. When he sacked his writers and decided to provide his own material audiences soon lost interest and in the end it all proved to be too much.

Ten years after being involved in *THE BLOOD DONOR.* I was directing a film in Australia. We were shooting a scene under Sydney Harbour bridge on a very hot day. I was working with an Australian crew who as usual were

doing an excellent job. At mid day when we stopped for lunch our Cameraman who had worked with me on several other films around the world showed me a copy of his morning paper. At the bottom of a page there was a story about someone we both knew. A man whose body had been found that morning surrounded by empty bottles of pills in a Sydney hotel. His name was Tony Hancock. After working with Hancock I went on to other things.
So too did the geniuses who had made their late lamented star a household name. Simpson and Galton went on to create many more memorable characters. In their next show - *STEPTOE AND SON* - they brought together Wilfrid Brambell and Harry H.Corbett - two talented actors who were very experienced but fundamentally quite different in their approach to life. Off screen they did not have much to talk about but with superb scripts and years of acting experience they were able to create characters that came to life in a very special way.
Two other actors who also had very different views were later to record shows in the same studio. When David Croft cast Arthur Lowe and John Le Mesurier in *DAD'S ARMY* he brought together two people who on screen could bring any scene to life. David, was one of the most brilliant producers of the day our time. He was also a very experienced writer who knew the everything there is to know about televising comedy. The many series he created included *ARE YOU BEING SERVED?,HI-DE-HI.* and a number of other notable successes. On *DADS ARMY* he worked with Jimmy Perry - an actor who had once been a Butlin's redcoat. They were a great team and the shows were transmitted at became peak times for nearly ten years. Eighty episodes were produced .The first was recorded in 1968 and they are still being repeated by television networks all over the world.

Arthur Lowe and John Le Mesurier, who played the two main parts, had very different personalities. When the series began Lowe had done a lot of stage work but he was not a particularly big name. He had also appeared for a while in *CORONATION STREET*. He was quite an ambitious man who preferred to do things his way. When filming on location the shooting schedule was tactfully arranged so it allowed time for him to have a full English breakfast and complete his early morning toilet arrangements before the unit set off for the first location. By contrast John Le Mesurier had appeared in countless feature films for years. Today the term "laid back" would describe him perfectly. He was one of those wonderfully relaxed good natured people who can appear to be taking no Interest in anything, and then effortlessly give a performance which steals the scene.

Many yeas later, when my mother died at the age of 95 and I was sorting out her papers, I discovered that she had written to Le Mesurier to tell him how much she enjoyed his work. He did not know her from Adam and he must have received thousands of letters from fans. Somehow he had managed to write a delightful hand written reply. It was a characteristically generous gesture and I am sure it must have been greatly appreciated at the time.

On screen Lowe and Le Mesurier worked brilliantly together but off screen they did not have much in common. Again the professionalism of Croft and his team turned a simple idea into a television classic. Today I doubt if that series could ever be made. Even when it started over thirty years ago, there was some opposition. Paul Fox, who as Controller of Programmes was then responsible for much of the final output of BBC television, was concerned that the series might be what today would be called politically correct. He was worried that viewers might think the BBC was making fun of Britain's armed forces. Meetings were held and all points of view were duly considered before Croft and his team were told to go ahead. I doubt if that would happen today and television will continue to lose out to DVDs and other forms of entertainment until the networks are again managed by people with the foresight and knowledge which BBC executives had in those days.

One of the last shows I worked on as BBC trainee has today become something of a cult. I had just finished my stint on *TONIGHT* and was about to go home. As the *TONIGHT* set was being dismantled I was told that the studio was going to used over the weekend to produce a pilot show for a new science fiction series. The pilot would be recorded on film for archive use only. Pilot programmes are test shows staged to find out if new ideas are likely to be worth developing. I was asked if I would come in over the weekend and edit the recording. As I had nothing planned, I readily agreed. When I arrived for work the following day the studio we had en working in had been transformed. It was a relatively small space. Lime Grove was old. The studios had Originally been used by Gainsborough Pictures in the 1930s. It was there that Alfred Hitchcock had shot some of his earliest films.

In the middle of the studio, where Cliff Michelmore and his team had presented *TONIGHT* the previous day, they had built a small set which looked as if it had been made with reject parts from a plastics factory. It had obviously been put created at rock bottom cost. I learned later that the budget for making the entire pilot programme was only £15,000.00. When I tell you that in 2008 the average budget for a thirty second commercial was £161,000. you will appreciate how things have changed.

In one corner of the set, for reasons I was then unable to understand there was a blue telephone of the type then used only by police. Various other strange objects were scattered around but nothing made much sense.

That evening I sat in the basement recording area and watched the show being recorded I began to realize what

it was all about. The show featured an actor who was then relatively unknown. He had just appeared as an army sergeant in a film shot at Pinewood studios - *CARRY ON SERGEANT!* The film was a relatively minor Rank production and not one of the celebrated Peter Rogers *CARRY ON SERIES* which started the following year. The actor's name was William Hartnell. In our Lime Grove studio he seemed to be rather bewildered. He was used to appearing in feature films where scenes are shot one at a time with a singe camera. There is plenty of time between each shot for actors to study their lines while the camera and lights are repositioned. In a television studio the production techniques are completely different. The action is often filmed from beginning to end straight through in one take. As the action proceeds a number of cameras ranged around the set simultaneously shoot different shots from different angles. In a control gallery the director and his team cut instantly from one camera to another . There is no pause between shots. Hartnell was clearly not really prepared for this and at times had difficulty remembering every line of what was
a fairly unintelligible script. To make life easier for him lines and cues were written in bold type on boards which were held on the edge of the set just out of shot. If he forgot a line he merely had to casually glance at a board to pick up the theme - a task he managed to do admirably. Eventually the recording session ended and we knew that the show was safely 'in the can'. The film was processed overnight ready for us to edit the
following day. At that point the recording was made for archive purposes only. No one thought it would ever be seen by the public but fortunately it was kept. And in case you want to know what the programme was called it was the very first episode of *DOCTOR WHO.*
After three years of training I was beginning to get restless, though I realised there was still quite a lot to learn. Thirty years later I am still learning and technology

is changing so quickly that I shall probably be lowered into my grave with a textbook in my hands. As a young man I was then much more ambitious, and the BBC's method of dealing with everything in a formal civil service manner made me impatient. I enjoyed the time I had spent making programmes and in three years had done what today could take ten to accomplish but I realised I had reached an impasse. Having trained us to meet the high standards they required, the BBC wanted to keep us working for them for as long as possible. I was offered an excellent salary and a full time contract, apparently for life - something that today no one would ever get. I turned them down because I had got restless. The BBC had its own ways of doing things. Those ways had to be respected and observed. Every year, each member of staff had an annual interview with his or her head of department. After the first two years some of the more adept bosses actually remembered who you were! The whole procedure was a complete farce, which anyone with the slightest intelligence found difficult to accept. With twenty two thousand employees, one sometimes felt that nobody cared. I started to consider my long-term aims and began to look around so I could decide what I wanted to do next. Independent commercially sponsored television was just starting and a number of colleagues had already left to explore pastures new. It was tempting to stay put in a well paid which I very much enjoyed but I have never been able to resist a challenge. At the age of twenty four I decide to resign from BBC and see what I could do. It was a tremendous gamble but it proved to be one of the best decisions I have made in my life.

3. BREAKING OUT

My first years in television had been great fun. When I eventually decided to resign and leave the BBC I had a nasty feeling that I might perhaps be putting a premature end to what so far had turned out to be quite a promising career. The 1960's and 70's were bad times for anyone trying to start any kind of business. During that time Britain was run by three different Prime Ministers. Harold Wilson was the first. He was followed by Jim Callaghan and Edward Heath as businesses struggled to survive. The government and trade unions were at war with each other almost continuously. In those days unions were often controlled by a handful of militants who had political objectives and wielded considerable power. At one point, when I was fighting to get my new business established, Britain was only working for three days each week. The rest of the time industry was so paralysed by strikes that nothing could be done. As a result interest rates reached an all time high and it was hard to find anyone with any confidence in the future. The unions held absolute power and closed shops were the order of the day. In the film business, if you did not have a union ticket you could not work in the industry at all. Nothing could be shot without a full union crew and that meant agreeing to hugely expensive over manning. Unless you worked for a major company it was almost impossible to get a union ticket. As companies were not allowed to employ anyone who did not already possess a ticket, getting into the industry as a newcomer was a challenging task! The unions held immense power and they misused it for years costing their members millions of pounds.

On one occasion I recall we were shooting a programme for the BBC in Kent. One of the scenes we filmed showed some people eating a meal inside a restaurant. In the distance, through the windows of the restaurant, one could just see people passing along a distant street. All the actors appearing in the scene had to have fully paid up union tickets. Every one of our fourteen man production team also had to be members of the technicians union. The background music we used in the scene had to be recorded my members of the musicians union. It was a stupid as that. I recall this scene particularly because it caused a major incident. Every morning cast and crew were taken to the location in a specially chartered bus. When filming ended the same bus brought everyone back to London. The shoot went well and when it ended the film moved into the cutting rooms in the usual way. As editing began I got a call from a union shop steward. He asked if I was aware than a non-union member had appeared in one of the scenes we had filmed. As we always went to great lengths to obey the rules and stick by union agreements the news came as a complete surprise.

On investigation we discovered that our coach driver, who had got bored hanging around while scenes were being filmed, had walked along a road which could just be seen through one of the windows in the restaurant. He was a long way away but, as he was wearing his bus diver's uniform his figure could just be seen when the shot was enlarged. A union activist in the cast had noticed the man and reported the incident to his shop steward. To re-shoot that scene would have cost thousands of pounds. We apologised for what had clearly been an oversight and hoped the union would recognise that the error had not been deliberate. They would not agree and told us that the production would be blacked until the offending shot was removed. As it could not be cut out with without making nonsense of the entire scene, we were faced with a serious dilemma. Discussions continued for several days during which all production work was halted. Eventually the union agreed for the shot to be shown if we promised to make a substantial contribution to "the union's benevolent fund." We had no option but to comply.

In today's more liberal world you may find situations like that are hard to believe. Then they were the norm and they made starting and running a business a much greater nightmare that it needed to be. Today militant union power is no longer a feature of everyday life and everyone benefits.

In the trendy 1960s union power was at its height. As teenagers listened to the Beatles and wore flared trousers I decided to leave the BBC to try and earn a living as an a independent producer of films and television programmes. Moving out to set up on my own was a difficult decision to make. I should not have worried for the move soon proved to be one of the best decisions I have made in the course of my life and it lead to many exciting adventures.

In the course of my training I had been able to work on a wide range of programmes at different stages of production. I had managed to acquire essential production skills by working with many of the best talents of the day. Now I wanted to do something on my own, but deciding what course to follow was clearly going to be a challenge. After a lot of agonising, I decided to try to make a short documentary in any spare time I could find during the last three months of my BBC contract. I would choose a subject, and prepare a script. I would then ave to shoot and edit it, and look after all the other stages of production without any outside help. I realised it could be a recipe for disaster but I had to prove to myself that the years I had spent watching and listening had taught me something I could benefit from. There was just one problem. I did not have any money.

Professional productions are not made for the cost of a few tins of beans. At that time, I was living on a diet of beans in order to have enough cash to join my friends in the bar. I knew that making any documentary was likely to cost far more than I possessed. There seemed to be two possibilities. I could borrow money from a bank or try to find a way of doing something very simple without any outside funds. When I discovered what bank interest rates were likely to be, the decision became much easier to make and I started to try to find a subject I could film for next to nothing.

Every would-be filmmaker has subjects he or she would like to film. Most of them are impractical for one reason or another. In my experience, when you are working with very limited resources, the secret is to keep it simple.

You have to avoid being too ambitious. Expensive actors, big production numbers and extravagant locations must all be forgotten. You must find a subject which can be filmed with limited equipment but it must be one which audiences will find is interesting to watch. You may then eventually be able to recover your costs by selling whatever you manage to produce. If that sounds easy, believe me, it is not! It took me a while to find a suitable theme and a lot longer to turn it into a film.

Artists have always interested me. The fact that they Create something out of nothing has always appealed. They also usually have clear views on what they like and dislike. They can explain what they do and why they do it, and that, to a filmmaker, is a definite asset. So I eventually decided that I would like to make a short film about any well known artist. The question was - who? Did I want to explore the work of a living artist or a dead one? Would my first production be on Turner or Michelangelo or on an artist who alive and working today? I visited galleries and read piles of books but could not find anything that inspired me. When I was beginning to give up hope of ever finding a subject which could be satisfactorily explored with my resources, I found myself visiting Coventry Cathedral. It had just been rebuilt after extensive war damage. Some of the finest artists of the day had been involved in the restoration work. As I entered via the west door I noticed that one wall consisted entirely of huge glass engravings. They showed life sized figures which had been beautifully etched on sheets of plate glass. As I walked past, the effect was amazing. The figures appeared to be watching me. They were very fine indeed and I wanted to know who had produced them so I asked the cathedral authorities. The information they provided led me to a tiny studio in North London and eventually gave me the subject for my first independently produced film.

John Hutton was born in New Zealand. A tall and modest man, he had pioneered new techniques for engraving glass. He used a small grinding wheel which was mounted on a flexible drive and attached to a dentist's drill. By moving it slowly across the surface of the glass and applying different pressures, he found he could cut deeply or shallowly into the glass and allow more or less light to pass through. As people walked past, the figures he created seemed to come to life .The effect was impressive but it was difficult to achieve. If he pressed too hard and generated too much heat, Hutton knew the glass would crack and months of work would instantly be destroyed. Fortunately he was highly skilled so that rarely happened. For. His work had been internationally admired but he had remained a quiet and modest man. When we first met I watched him at work and explained that I would like to make a film about his technique and what he had achieved. The Coventry commission would form part of it. The film would also look at work he had done for the Shakespeare Trust and a number of the commissions he had completed elsewhere. I instinctively knew that this was the subject I had been looking for. Hutton was an interesting and a very expressive man. He had pioneered new techniques and everything he did took place in one room. That meant that from a film point of view I would only need a simple camera and very few lights. I also realised that I was facing a top international artist who could command

Substantial fees, which I could not afford. I decided the only thing to do was to be completely honest.

At our first meeting I explained my situation.

" I like your work and would love to make film about what you are doling but I cannot afford to pay you a fee because I haven't got any money."

I explained that I had just completed a BBC training course and that this would be my first independent professional production. I would have to borrow the equipment I needed and take a lot of short cuts to make anything at all.

I expected to be thrown out there and then but Hutton was not that sort of man. He recalled how he himself had started, with a few ideas and no commercial backing, and kindly agreed to give me his time and a free hand, if I could complete my filming in a couple of days.

I spent the next week arranging to borrow a clockwork 16mm camera from one good friend and trying to persuade another to process the out-of-date government film stock I had had managed to buy at a knock-down price. Lights were obtained for the price of a few pints of beer and I was eventually ready to start shooting.

For two days I filmed everything Hutton did. I then spent a week visiting some of the jobs he had already completed. Finally I sat and talked to him at length, recording our conversation on a borrowed tape recorder. As he explained how he worked and talked about his background and his plans for the future, the basis of a film began to emerge.

Over the next few weeks I managed to hire a film cutting room and edit the material I had shot. I worked at night, when I had finished my BBC commitments. The lessons I had learned over the previous years began to make sense and I ended up with a final edited version which at last was ready for showing. I felt it was adequate but was not entirely satisfied. I have never been totally satisfied with anything I have produced, but others gave me courage. When I showed the film to a group of my colleagues, they were much kinder than I had dared to hope. At least I had done what I set out to do.

In the last month of my BBC contract I found I was particularly busy, so I had to put any further ambitions aside. Friends suggested I should send the Hutton film to some television sales agents and see if they could help me to recover my costs. I sent a copy off and in due course received a distribution contract. It was signed and returned and I tried to put the film out of my mind.

Many months later I received another letter enclosing a cheque for a thousand pounds and telling me that my film had been sold to the main television networks in Australia and Canada. It had also won an award in a Canadian film festival. The last paragraph of the letter explained that the film was currently being assessed by another television network which turned out to be the BBC! . Six months later the film was one of the first to be transmitted on what was then the Corporation's brand new channel - BBC2. It was a success I had not even dared to hope for. With all the audacity and ignorance of youth I, left the BBC when my contract expired and set out to woo the world a Independent Producer.

3. GOING SOLO

When I left, the BBC's permanent staff was reduced to twenty-two thousand, nine hundred and ninety nine. I felt a twinge of guilt but, as their chances of survival were better than mine, it soon passed. My main concern was what to do next. I knew my objectives but how could I achieve them? I knew nothing about business and needed some advice so I decided to call on our family solicitor. He had what my father always described as 'family connections' which I found out actually meant that he was a cousin of someone who had married a distant relative many years ago. His office was in London. He had been there for years and I assumed he would be able to tell me all I needed to know about setting up a business. Full of confidence, I set off to see him.

"Cousin Harold," as my father always referred to him, worked in a small office in the heart of the city. It was a listed ancient monument, and it suited him perfectly. Inside and out nothing had changed for years. There had been the odd startling decision. In 1985, twenty years after everyone else, Harold had abandoned the bowler hat he wore on his daily walk from the station to his office. Apart from that, there had been no changes for as long as anyone could recall. His office was straight out of a Dickens novel. Papers covered every available surface and a couple of faded prints hung above the fireplace ,where an ancient gas fire hissed contentedly.

"Come in, dear boy," he said as he rose to welcome me knocking over boxes of files which crashed to the floor. "It may look a mess but I know where everything is and that's what matters these days. Don't you agree?"

He pointed to a battered armchair.

"You have been here some time?" I enquired.

"Forty years next month," Harold replied adding "And they are still trying to increase the rent. I'm on a fixed tenancy you know, and they are always trying to get me out. Want to build one of those burger places. No respect for anyone or anything nowadays. Personally I've always been perfectly happy with a cheese roll."

I had hoped to meet one of the city's leading figures - a solicitor who provided successful companies with cutting edge advice. In stead I found myself facing an old man who appeared to have spent the last forty years sorting out long-term legal squabbles and battling with a number of city corporations.

"Don't get too big - that's the secret,'" he roared, briefly springing to life. "And never allow yourself to become a corporation. They don't know what they're doing most of the time. Dear Sir and yours faithfully- .That's their level. They write memos to each other day after day. I've seen it all so remember what I say. Stay small . That's my advice."

With a bank balance almost down to single figures, there was little prospect of my doing anything else. We chatted for half an hour and Harold continued to tell me what was wrong with life. He wanted to be helpful but when I left his office my future was as uncertain as it was when I arrived. I desperately needed to make some money. I eventually made around £2,000.00 from sales of the Hutton film. As the entire production had been made for about £150.00 I was delighted with the return on my limited investment but I realised that it would not be enough to start a business. With no other course to follow I decided to go and see my bank.

The newly appointed manager has been in his job for a couple of weeks. When his predecessor had retired after managing the branch for years, the young man who faced me had been promoted and given his job. He was slightly older than me and it soon became clear that he had been trained to sell all the banks services as vigorously as possible. He was more interested in his own future than he could ever be in mine.

"It's a difficult job today, managing a bank" he confided as soon as I arrived.
"We are set targets which we have to reach each month. We have to sell pensions, insurance and all the bank's services and give our customers the best possible rate."
My heart bled for him and my confidence sank to new depths. I eventually managed to explain what I wanted to do but as soon as I finished he returned to the attack.
" Yes. I can see it now. You with your will be producing all the west end shows." He smiled and continued, with the briefest pause for breath.
"You will need insurance for yourself and your staff. You will also need a pension for when you retire. If I can just jot down the details I am sure we can offer you a very good rate."
It was clearly going to be a wasted half-hour.
He delivered the sales message he had learned at training school while I counted the gold motifs on the wallpaper in his office . We did not share a single objective. His goals and mine were far apart. In a fit of generosity he did finally agree to offer me a limited overdraft for three
months, but that was the most I was going to get. Lending money to young people with ideas but no security was clearly not part of his brief.
When you are short of money it is surprising how strong the urge to work can be. It was becoming abundantly clear that, if I did not find something to boost my ever dwindling funds, my future was more likely to be in the dole queue than anywhere in television. When things were beginning to look grim I got a phone call from the last organisation I expected to hear from - my former employers - BBC. Television.
My caller reminded me that we had worked together in my BBC days. He then went on to explain:
" We have just bought a series of programmes which were produced in Belgium. The only problem is that they are all in French. The people we normally use to sort out

these things are very busy. I don't suppose you could give us a hand?"

The request for help could not have come at a better time. It meant translating and dubbing eight, thirty minute shows. In practical terms that would mean several weeks' work and a some much needed cash. I wanted the job but did not want to sound too eager.

To my astonishment I found myself saying, "I would love to help but I'm running my own business now and I would need to be on BBC's list of approved contractors." For a few seconds there was silence and I thought I had lost my chance then I heard the magic words -
"I think we could manage that. After all you worked for us for several years and you were alright then."

Two weeks later the films arrived and I started by first independent contract, making English versions of Belgian television programmes for the BBC.

I had learned about foreign dubbing when I was a full time member of the BBC's staff. The Corporation had recently produced a series of dramatisations of some of George Simenon's MAIGRET novels. When they were proved popular in the UK a number of overseas television networks wanted to acquire the rights to show the programmes in their own countries. One of the first to express an interest was Germany. With very little notice, I was asked if I and a colleague would supervise the preparation of a German language versions at the Bavarian film studios in Munich.

By what must have presumably have been an oversight, the BBC booked us into the best hotel in town. It had a world wide reputation for luxury and service. We were delighted with our good fortune and hoped that the work would last for months. Translating and dubbing films from one language to another is a particular skill which some countries are better at than others. Words have to be translated so they make sense, sound completely natural and take the same time to read as the original dialogue. If

a translation is bad actors doing the re-voicing will be unable to make their lip movements precisely match those of the original actors seen on the screen. It is job that calls for a number of different skills and the Germans had years of experience of doing it to perfection.
We largely left it to the experts. From time to time we helped by providing them with music and sound effects tracks. It all seemed to be going to plan and in the studio at least everyone was pleased with the progress that was being made. Back in London however it was a different story. The bills for our hotel accommodation were coming in and they were apparently giving those responsible for the production budget many sleepless nights. They could not understand why the charges were so high. After a couple of weeks they decided to send a management consultant to Munich to see what was going on.
In due course a middle aged man in an old crumpled suit arrived on what he told us was his first overseas trip. He was employed by an independent firm of consultants who at that time were doing various cost audits for the BBC. He knew nothing at all about film, television or dubbing and was completely out of his depth. One his first day in town he joined us for dinner in our five star hotel. He struggled with some prawns and a well done steak and chips while we forced ourselves to eat a magnificent five course dinner. He even managed to drink his finger bowl thinking it was soup. His visit lasted two days and then he returned to base never to be seen or heard of again.
After a year of full time self employment things were beginning to take off. With money coming in, at last I could afford to make plans for the future. I still did not have an office or any of the things businesses normally enjoy, but I did have orders worth several thousand pounds and that was good enough for me. I started to put together what banks would now call a business plan. It encouraged me to decide what I wanted to do.

I knew I wanted to produce films and television shows but realised that feature films for cinema showing would be beyond my reach financially. That left making television programmes and exploring the potentially lucrative market for corporate public relations and training films and it was those areas that I decided to explore.

With money coming in, I decided it was time to try advertising. For the first and only time in my life I put an advertisement in *The Financial Times*. After numerous phone calls trying to chat up lovely ladies in their advertising department, I eventually managed to get my two-inch column ad. in what I thought would be a prominent position. It cost, what to me then was a small fortune and it modestly announced that my new company was available to make films for sponsors who wanted the best.

That advertisement taught me the first rule of advertising. It produced just one reply. It was from a company that made plastic sheet film to stick on the roofs of conservatories. They wondered if they could interest me in their products! Rule one, as I had just discovered, is to choose the right medium for the market you want to do business in. I had made the first of the many mistakes which were to come.

Fortunately orders were now coming in. The dear old BBC soon offered me another job. They had succeeded in selling the first twenty six *DR.WHO* programmes to an overseas buyer. They had signed contracts and then discovered that the musicians who had recorded some of the music used on the original UK soundtrack, would not allow it to be used overseas. All 26 soundtracks had to be re-created with new sound effects, different music (which was copyright clearable) and scripts which were ready for foreign language dubbing. The whole task was placed in my hands and I and a number of hastily recruited colleagues, spent several weeks creating explosions, footsteps, electronic effects and hundreds of other sounds many of which are still used today.

By the time that job was finished I was beginning to feel and almost talk like a Dalek but the need to make enough money to keep the business going soon brought me down to earth. Much to my surprise I was making money and I was thoroughly enjoying what I was doing. The BBC had got me off to an excellent start but now enquiries
Were coming in from other parties. They came from a variety of sources. A friend of a friend had heard that I worked in television. He was an engineer and at that time he was working on the test programme for a new jet aircraft. His company had just staged what they described as "ditching tests" to find out what would happen if there was an emergency and their new plane had to crash in the sea. They used scale model aircraft and a very large tank and had arranged for the tests to be filmed by a local wedding photographer when he happened to be free.
The results were not impressive and I was asked to edit the film and add a professionally recorded soundtrack which would make the pictures more interesting to watch. The aircraft being tested became a very successful passenger jet carrying around 250 people. The directors of the company were delighted with the film and immediately offered me another commission which to change my life once again. It was a job I nearly lost before it began.

The man who eventually gave me a contract was the sales director of what was then one of biggest producers of aircraft and military equipment in the world. He was used to dealing with high flyers in every sense. His suppliers were all huge companies which had become household names. Naturally he always expected the best. When he saw the work I had done on his ditching film he liked what he saw. He also assumed it had been made by a large company with resources like his own. The reality, as he was about to discover, was a very different story.

At that time I was beginning to realise that I could no longer continue to operate from home. An office of one kind or another had become essential. As money was still in short supply I decided to rent an accommodation address. I shopped around and eventually found an organisation which operated from the top floor of a building in Regent Street - one of London's most prestigious streets. The address was a good one and the services the company offered seemed just right for me.

For a modest monthly fee they would hold my mail for collection and take any telephone messages people which people cared to leave. This of course was years before mobile phones were invented and at the time it was not easy to keep in touch with people who were on the move. They also had one fully furnished office which could be hired on an hourly or a daily basis to enhance the basic service and make it seem even more impressive. The charges were reasonable and the address carried prestige so I decided to sign up.

The Regent street address worked well for me for several months. No one ever wanted to pay me a visit, so my potential customers were blissfully unaware that the film company writing to them from the heart of London was a one-man band with plenty of experience but very few assets. I saw no reason why that situation should not continue until I could collect enough funds to expand. Everything was going well until one morning the phone rang with an unexpected call. The aircraft company's sales director wanted to come and see me to discuss an important new project which he had in mind.

"Would tomorrow be convenient?" he enquired. As I could not think of any excuse we arranged to meet the following day. At twelve o'clock precisely an expensive chauffeur driven car drew up outside. I had ironed my one and only suit and stood in the street waiting. Sir Colin (not his real name) was one of British industry's top men and I soon found out why. He was quick thinking, ruthless and very direct. I had already decided that the only way to deal with the situation was to be completely honest. As the chauffeur closed the doors of his car I explained that I only rented space in part of the building and that the area I used was on the top floor. Sir Colin nodded politely and we both moved inside.

Unfortunately on that day the lift had broken down.

I explained that this was frequently a problem and the landlords had promised to replace the lift as soon as they could.

"But not today presumably", Sir Colin muttered as we started to climb ten flights of stairs. It says much for him that we were still on speaking terms by the time we reached the top.

In the supplementary office, which I had splashed out and hired for an hour and a half, we had a brief discussion and then we adjourned for lunch. As the meal progressed he told me about a major contract which his company had just won. It was for work to be done in Saudi Arabia. The contract required a filmed record to be made at every stage.

" Is this the sort of thing you might be interested in doing," Sir Colin asked as he paid for the lunch.

You will not be surprised to know that I told him it was! Saudi Arabia is one of the richest countries in the world. It is also, as anyone who has worked there will tell you, a place where they have their own way of doing things. Everything must be done the Saudi way and the rest of the world is expected to conform. You can only work in the country by invitation. The Saudi Arabian government has to be contacted by an approved contractor and your entry into the kingdom has to be authorised before a visa can be issued. That can take weeks,months or even longer. When an application is eventually approved you can set off, as I and various colleagues have done many times on Saudi Air flights.

Like most Arab counties, Saudi Arabia is dry. Alcohol is banned and that ban extends to the national airline, so everyone arrives stone cold sober. Saudi Air has a huge fleet of the world's latest aircraft and the standard of service on international routes is usually quite high. On my first visit we landed at Jeddah airport a few minutes ahead of time. We taxied in and stopped in front of a very small building where our aircraft waited for a considerable time. Nothing seemed to be happening and nobody moved in the section of the aircraft which I and two colleagues we were travelling in.

"This is the Royal terminal," a stewardess eventually explained. "Only members of the Royal Family and VIP guests are allowed out here. We were intrigued. Had we been travelling with the King himself or with someone else of world renown? We sat there and waited for half an hour and then at last a handful of men in blazers started to get off. The stewardess was again able to explain. Apparently our aircraft was carrying a cricket team which had been invited to the country by one of the country's many Crown Princes. They must alight first, and until their host was ready to receive them no one else could leave the aircraft. We waited for another half an hour once again regretting the absence of a bar.

When the cricketers had hone we prepared to follow but we did not get very far. A further announcement explained why" The aircraft will now proceed to the International terminal where all passengers will then be able to get off" we were advised.

Three hours later we joined a long queue for customs. It was an interesting introduction to a country where patience is not a virtue. It is a necessity.

Our first day in Saudi ended on a better note. I had been concerned that the accommodation we would be offered might be rather basic. Fears of sleeping in a desert hammock under the stars had filled my mind, but they proved to be unfounded. We were driven to a five-star hotel. It was one of the best I have encountered. It was superbly managed by Swiss interests and served the best international cuisine. As I fell asleep in a huge double bed, I was intrigued to learn that the Ugandan tyrant and dictator Idi Amin, was living in a luxury suite on the floor above.

A few days after our arrival I was instructed to report to the local Sheikh, responsible for the area where we hoped much of our filming would eventually take place.

A state of the art Japanese four-wheel drive vehicle, driven by a Turkish chauffeur, arrived to collect me at the appointed hour. He did not speak English. I do not speak Turkish, so we got along famously. For four hours we drove out across the desert.

We seemed to be going from nowhere to nowhere at considerable speed. I was beginning to think we were completely lost when a large white building appeared on the horizon. The driver set course to drive up to it. Ten minutes later we stopped in front of what I can only describe as a derelict Walt Disney fairytale castle. It looked as if a corner of Disney World had been uprooted and dumped in the desert. Crumpled towers and turrets which had collapsed, stood at each corner. The whole area seemed to be completely barren. I could not imagine how anyone could want to live in such a derelict place.

The car stopped and I opened a door and started to get out, clutching the only thing I had brought with me - a rather battered briefcase. Before I could say anything my Turkish companion slammed the door and drove off. I had a nightmare vision of being left alone to die in what I felt sure was an empty desert.

As there was nothing else to do I trudged through the sand towards the faded whitewashed castle. The one possible entrance appeared to be blocked, but alongside it there was an outdoor staircase. On one side it had partly collapsed but as there appeared to be no other way of entering the building I started to climb the steeply angled steps which remained in tact. At the top my progress was blocked by a filthy red curtain which I drew back to reveal a sight I shall never forget.

I found myself at the end of a very long room. It was quite dark and sparsely furnished. A single table stood in the middle but round every wall there were the most luxurious armchairs you could ever imagine. They could have been bought at Harrods. Sitting in the chairs were the smartest group of Arabs I had yet seen. They were all in full ceremonial dress, complete with swords. A deep pile carpet covered the floor. It lay as it had been rolled out many years before. The edges had never been fixed. It was a dazzling sight and I stood for a few moments totally transfixed . Before I could make any other move a a young Arab rose from a seat nearby. In impeccable English he said, "Good morning Mr. Burder. You are very welcome here." I later learned that he had spent two years at the Royal Military Academy, Sandhurst.

To confirm my welcome, with much ceremony, a can of Coca-Cola was produced. I was then invited to Explain why I wanted to film.

As I spoke my words were translated to Arabic When I finished the young man explained that the people in the room were all the local VIPs who between them controlled the entire district. We shook hands, smiled and got on well. In an hour of discussion much was achieved. I got permission to film things which had never been filmed before and heard about a new city they were planning to build. It was an excellent way of establishing many useful contacts.

In the years which followed, I filmed in Saudi Arabia many times. We were able to make films about some of their biggest achievements and, as work progressed, I was able to get to know the people of this immensely wealthy kingdom a little better and I came to like them very much. Over the years I have filmed in many Arab states and in Israel. I have always been treated with courtesy and have made many Jewish and Arab friends whose company and ways of life I enjoy and respect. It is a pity George Bush was unable to get his act together and consider the ordinary people of the world who are sometimes rich and often poor but, if you take the trouble to get to know them, can sometimes be a pleasure to know.

Returning to London after my fist visit I found it quite difficult to get back to a normal routine. I was driven to Jeddah airport from the middle of the desert which at that time, long before satellites and mobile phones, was 250 miles from the nearest phone. The journey took most of a night. At one point my driver had screeched to a halt just in time to avoid colliding with a camel. The following day the short journey from Heathrow airport to central London in the rush hour soon brought me down to earth once again.

In my absence my telephone answering service had taken quite a lot of calls and new business was rolling in, so I felt that perhaps it was time for a modest expansion. I realised that I was going to need a full time secretary and set out to find one. In those days, before computers secretaries had to work a lot harder than they ever do now. If an error was made when a document was being typed there were no keys you could press top correct the fault. The whole document had to be typed again. You had to know what you were doing and the three secretaries I employed in the first twenty years of running my business certainly did. They were all superb. I could never have survived without them but they were difficult to find. The first was Margaret Sylvester who came to me after working in a hospital. She had the conscientious approach to work which today is so difficult to find. Her typing was accurate and fast - both essential qualities then as today, and dealt with an ever growing procession of callers. Her personality set everyone at ease and she took a lot of problems off my shoulders. Most secretaries, when they apply for jobs in

films, expect to join a world of glamour. They see themselves welcoming stars and sitting in the spotlight. Maggie was wonderfully down-to-earth and had the sense to realise that running a film company is just the same as running any other business. It's hard work and there is inevitably quite a lot of repetition. She became adept at banishing salesmen and telling people I was in a meeting when I was probably in a pub. We were one of the first businesses to invest in new technology. We bought one of the first word processors. It was a huge machine which stood on the floor and took up quite a lot of space. Maggie would type a single line of text. The machine would record and display it on a one-line screen. When she pressed a button the machine made purring noises and recorded the line in its innermost guts. When a complete page was ready, it sounded an alarm. Another button was then pressed and more wheels whirred. The whole machine shook and one page of something resembling the input text finally emerged. It looked quite impressive but it cost a fortune and it did not really achieve very much. When the first computers arrived it was sold for scrap and we moved on to our
next high tech disaster - one of the first telephone answering machines.

At that time, for reasons I never understood, it was actually illegal to buy an answering machine. An obscure regulation, presumably introduced to safeguard their monopoly the telephone company decreed that machines could only be leased or hired. One of the first mistakes I made was to sign a five-year rental agreement for the machine we acquired. It was the best machine at the time but far better models were soon introduced and we were locked into equipment we could not replace. In those days people were not used to talking to machines. Most rang off the moment their call was answered. As time progressed, the less timid started to leave messages. Some spoke in a formal way like BBC announcers. Others, who

were not sure if they were being recorded, would preface their remarks by saying "If you can hear this I just want to Say..." and then ramble on.
Our most interesting caller rang us at much the same time every day. We never knew who he as because when the machine answered he just breathed very loudly into the mouthpiece for several minutes and then went away.
As business increased, it became clear that I was going to need an accountant to look after the books. As two and two have always added up to five in my way of Calculating things, it seemed a good idea to try to find someone who could at least sort out the tax bills I was beginning to receive. I went to see an old established family firm recommended to me by a colleague in the BBC.
"Go and Uncle George," he had advised adding, "He's been doing it for ears and he must know everything there is to know by now." I took his advice and set out for his office in Bournemouth.
Today Bournemouth is a vibrant seaside town. It has an excellent university, an international conference centre and a good selection of fine hotels and restaurants. As Brighton has become more expensive and overcrowded, shrewd investors have moved further down the coast and brought new life to what has always been a very attractive place. The population today is a good mix of people of all ages and outlooks and Bournemouth is rapidly becoming the "in" place to be. In the 1960s it was quite a different story. Then the town had the tarnished image of a fading holiday resort. In his brilliant play *SEPARATE TABLES,* Terence Rattigan captured the atmosphere of the time.
As I travelled by train from London I studied a brochure which explained that development of the town had started around the turn of the century. The oldest building in Bournemouth has been there for was just over a hundred years.

I think Uncle George must have been there when it was built.

If age means experience he should have had a wealth of knowledge to impart. Alas when we met his memory had gone. When I reached his door, he spent several minutes trying to recall who I was and why I was there. He decided to check his diary and spent the next ten minutes trying to find it. His filing system was very like the family solicitor whose advice I had sought a few weeks before. His policy appeared to be to stack papers on every available surface and then use the floor.

" There's one thing you must always remember," he then advised. "Don't give them anything. They are all thieves and vagabonds! You must never help in any way!"

It was such an unexpected outburst I was taken aback. "Thieves and vagabonds?" I muttered. "Who exactly is it you are you talking about?" I timidly enquired

His reply was instant. "The Revenue of course! Damned tax inspectors. Robbers and thieves every one of them!" His face flushed with rage and I thought that at any minute he would have a seizure but I need not have worried He was used to it. The tirade was well rehearsed and delivered with conviction. I eventually managed to tear myself away. It had been an interesting experience but somehow I did not feel I had met quite the right man to manage my accounts.

Two weeks later I enlisted the help of a large city firm. Their operation was quite different. I met one of the firm's partners over lunch. It was an extravagant affair, which he paid for. It was about the only benefit I ever encountered during the three years in which they audited my accounts. I had planned to return the compliment and invite my host to dine with me but I discovered that the partner's time would be charged to me at £100 an hour. That was one lunch which never took place.

As many small businesses have discovered to their cost, large accountancy firms are nor really interested in what their small clients do. They have their systems and want everything to be channelled through them. Big companies are usually quite happy to comply. As they spend a large part of their lives pushing bits of paper from one department to another, they are able to cope. Staff can be delegated to re arrange books to meet the accountants' requirements, and no one worries about the costs involved. My colleagues and I were running a small business but we were actually quite efficient. We knew exactly what we were spending and what we were making. Having to present our figures under lots of totally irrelevant headings to comply with their systems did not exactly fill me with joy. They sent one of their Partners to see us from time to time but the firm's new recruits did most of the work. Young trainee accountants who were learning their jobs by auditing our accounts. It was an expensive arrangement with no obvious advantages, but we were getting busy and I did not have the time to look for anyone else. It was several years before I found an accountant who had forsaken another large city firm and set up on his own. He was well qualified, honest and extremely hard-working. His accounts made sense, and I am happy to report that he still acts for us today.

With business starting to roll in, I decided it was time to buy a car. For some time I had been driving a twenty year old wreck which had been a museum piece when I bought it when I first moved to London . It had a number of fundamental faults. The steering mechanism had to be packed with grease or the car would over-steer and land you in a ditch. My particular model was quite unique. It had all the original features, like the one I have just described, and ninety thousand miles on the clock. I had bought it at a very plush garage. The forecourt was lined with Mercedes and Jaguars. I looked at them enviously and then went in to ask what they cost. It was then that I met the formidable Miss Burrows.

If you can imagine a large lady in her mid-forties,

formally dressed in black with a large wide-brimmed hat, you can see Miss Burrows. She was the last person one would ever expect to find in charge of car sales in a garage. She beamed as I approached and her smile became even wider when I told her I wanted to buy a car. We went outside again to look again at all the models I had just inspected. Beaming from ear to ear she described the different models and listed their many apparently irresistible features. There was only one problem and that was plain to see . It was the price of every car she mentioned. It was far too high for the pittance I was earning. Half-an-hour later it was clear we had reached an impasse. I was preparing to leave when I noticed a small green and black car on the edge of the forecourt. "Is that one for sale?" I hesitantly asked.
"We have just taken it in part exchange," Miss Burrows replied. "It's very old and there would of course be no guarantee, but if you want it I suppose we could let you have it for the amount we have paid." That figure is still engraved on my soul. "It will cost you sixty-eight pounds."
I did not hesitate and became the proud owner of one of the oldest surviving Morris Tens which my friends promptly named "Foggy" after the blue haze of burning oil which seeped through the floor. It proved to be an interesting investment. In the first week I think I established a new world record for punctures to the mile. The tyres went flat almost everywhere I went. Further investments in new inner tubes managed to remedy that, but the problems with the brakes were harder to combat. The hand brake never worked and the foot brake only functioned if I slammed my foot hard against the floor and prayed.
I became quite adept at timing my progress up hills. I knew I could not stop and tried to wait till there was no one else around. It was risky but I was young. M.O.T tests did not exist and motoring was still fun. When I had

run the car for a year I repainted it by hand - a disaster I would not recommend.

As business increased I decided to try to trade it in against a newer car. I returned full of confidence to see Miss Burrows. I explained what I wanted to do and asked what she would allow me in part exchange. She walked round the car, inspecting it from every angle. After a long pause she made her offer.

"I could probably give you a packet of cigarettes."

A few weeks later I advertised Foggy in the London *Evening Standard*. I had just one reply. It was from a very pretty girl who came to see the car that very day. I explained that it was old and had done quite a high mileage so it was being sold on the basis of being seen, tried and tested. I could not give any guarantee. I offered to take her for a ride (in the car!) and asked where she would like to go.

"The Tower of London," she announced, which seemed strangely appropriate at the time. We set off through London's rush hour traffic and Foggy behaved beautifully, as she usually did when you knew how to deal with the many features which were not covered in the handbook. The girl was entranced and agreed to pay the price I had asked. It was £68. As Miss Burrows would have said - a real bargain!

Several years later I had made enough money to invest in a brand new car. I decided to buy a mini. The Austin and Morris minis had just come on the market for the first time and they were causing quite a stir. I believe they were the first vehicles to be fitted with transverse engines and other revolutionary new features. A few weeks after I had bought the car, I travelled to Longbridge to visit the factory where it had been built. I had arranged to shoot a few shots of designers at work for use in a motoring film I was planning to make. Alec Issigonis- the chief designer and one of the biggest names in car design- came out to meet me. Today Mr

Issigonis's place in the history of motoring is assured, but he was not a grand figure or a man who even seemed aware of his own success. I was 23 and knew absolutely nothing. He was at the peak of his career. I explained that I would like to take a few shots showing him at work on his designs for the mini. He immediately agreed and showed me to his office. There were no computers . He used a conventional drawing board like the ones I had used at school. In adjacent offices teams of draughtsmen developed his concepts and started a new motoring age. Nowadays computers try to do what he did. As a result many cars look much the same. Individuality and style are rare, and usually expensive. Issigonis had ideas and imagination. When he watched me unload four big lights and boxes of camera gear from the boot of the mini I had bought he beamed from ear to ear and told me that he was glad I had found enough space to carry everything I required.

I only spent an hour with him, but it was an hour I have remembered for forty years.

Moving equipment from place to place could sometimes be a problem. At that time I did not own anything at all. Lights and cameras were hired by the day and cutting rooms booked on an hourly basis. Lighting equipment tended to be bulky and in those days you needed a lot of lights to be able to film indoors. In the BBC one simply had to pick up a phone and ring the appropriate department.

If you wanted to send a can of film from one place top another you only had to pick up a phone. In BBC language you then asked for a "D.R." The Corporation loves using initials instead of words so someone can earn a living explaining what they mean. "D.R." simply stood for despatch rider.

The BBC had its own delivery service but it only employed a few staff, so requests for help were usually answered by the arrival of a London taxi. At one point I think the Corporation must have been employing half the taxis on London's streets for the demand was brisk around the clock. Years later, when they eventually added up the cost, I believe that arrangement was changed.

Working "outside," as I was beginning to discover, was An entirely different matter. If you wanted anything , you had to organise it yourself and pay for it with your own money. A great way to learn what budgets are all about. Setting up a new production the same rules applied. In the BBC, if I wanted to film at a particular location, there was always someone one I could call who would know what to do. Working "outside" was not the same at all.

The letters "BBC" open doors, and that applies all over the world. I had enjoyed that advantage for several years, without realising how valuable it was it until I left. If we wanted to shoot an interview in Trafalgar Square, a quick phone call to the appropriate government department would eliminate the need for reams of paperwork and ensure that all went smoothly the moment we arrived. As an independent producer I had to get permission from a host of departments and individuals most of which did not want to know. Having filmed round the world for many years, I regret to say that I have encountered more petty officials in London than anywhere else. If you set up the smallest tripod in a royal park you are likely to end up in the Tower. If you fail to carry the right form, signed by a suitable minion, you are liable to be beheaded at dawn! Britain loses millions of pounds a year from film-makers who prefer to shoot in places where the authorities are less petty and more helpful. If you are filming in a public place you will also have to deal with unexpected hazards. You may perhaps be filming a complicated shot which has taken you weeks to set up. All is going well. The camera is rolling and the subject you are shooting is giving the performance of your dreams, then a complete stranger walks into shot." Excuse me!" he says. "Are we on telly?"

You splutter "Cut!" and try to subdue the urge to strangle the man, who has unconsciously has ruined a really good take. You want to hang him from the nearest lamppost but you have to be polite. You answer his query and endeavour to persuade him to remain behind the barriers you have spent two days erecting, while you retake the scene. When the next take is ruined when an actor forgets his lines and it starts to rain at the start of take three, you begin to wonder why you ever shoot on location at all.

Documentary filming is sometimes simpler than trying to stage dramatic scenes on location, but not always. If you set up a camera and start filming you will attract any local idiots in a remarkably short time, and they can be difficult to disperse. I shall always recall trying to film an interview with a very pompous politician while a drunk who was convinced he was Napoleon kept popping up and down a few feet away. The MP wore an expensive suit and the interloper a tattered uniform with a cocked hat, but in their determination to appear in front of the camera they had much in common.

Some people will go to any lengths to avoid being filmed. Others will agree to take part and then shut up completely the moment the camera turns. The way people dress is sometimes a guide to the views they will express, but even that clue is not foolproof. I was once filmed some interviews in the streets of Chelsea - one of London's smarter areas- for a programme on life in Britain today. There were some very elegant people wandering around and one who I particularly recall. She was in her early forties and smartly dressed. When I asked for her views she spent some time telling me why she felt it was sad that money was now the only thing that mattered and traditional moral values were being ignored.

About a week later I found myself travelling on a bus in the same part of town. The lady we had filmed, still elegantly dressed, got on and sat beside me. She did not recognise me and I did not say anything to her, which was probably just as well. As the journey progressed she produced a newspaper and a pen, and then proceeded to enhance the printed photographs with the sort of additions you would be more likely to find on a lavatory wall.

My efforts at filming in Kensington and Chelsea have more than once produced unexpected results. A few years after the episode I have just described, we were shooting in Kensington gardens, quite near the Royal Palace where Princess Diana then lived. To set the scene we aimed to get a few pretty pictures of children playing with dogs and feeding the ducks on a pond.

It was a picture postcard setting and everyone seemed to be having a wonderful time. As one of the secrets of successful filming in public areas is to keep the camera hidden for as long as you can, we sat on a bench and waited hoping to see something which would capture the atmosphere of this idyllic spot. We did wait long. As we looked out across the pond, a nanny with two young children started to walk towards us. The children were dressed in clothes which the best costume designer in the world could not have surpassed. A delightful little girl, with a pom-pom on her hat, and a small boy in an elegant coat. We lined up our camera and waited as nanny produced a bag of crumbs and told the children to feed the birds. Some ducks approached and they all leaned forward, with crumbs in their hands. At exactly the same moment. a huge dog which was ambling past stopped right behind them. With great precision it lifted a leg and peed all over the children's elegant clothes and they never noticed! We had captured the whole scene on film and were shaking with laughter but it gave us a dilemma. Should I approach the nanny and explain what had happened? If I did, would she believe me? I am afraid I decided that discretion was the best course to adopt, and we retreated without spoiling their enjoyment. I often

wonder what happened when they got home.
Weeks later I found myself in a similar predicament. We were making a farming programme. One sequence showed a new tractor being used to spread muck over a large field. We chose our camera position carefully and filmed some very pleasant shots. As we captured our last scene, the direction of the wind suddenly changed and the raw sewage, which was destined for the crops, poured down on to us. We did our best to wash it off but the smell remained. When I went home by train that night, I took my usual seat but as the journey progressed I noticed that my fellow passengers were leaving the carriage one by one. The compartment was nearly empty when the train reached my stop!
The incidents I have just described took place on productions I was involved in when the business was beginning to get established. When I first started, getting any work at all was a major challenge. I spent every spare minute writing letters to companies trying to persuade them to make films with me. My requests met with a very mixed response. Most of my letters received no reply at all. Of those who did respond around 90% sent a stereotyped note promising that my letter would be kept on file. Others wrote to tell me they were quite happy with the film-making arrangements they already had. The majority just ignored me and as time passed I sometimes found myself wondering if my newly established business would ever really get off the ground. The Saudi experience had brought in some useful cash and there had been a number of small editing jobs. I had been able to pay the bills, but I had not yet been able to get the production work I wanted to do. With no track record, no equipment and very little money, as my bank manager had correctly surmised, the future was not looking particularly bright.
At last, when I was almost beginning to give up hope, one of my sales letters produced an encouraging reply. I

had written to the advertising manager of one of the best known brands of Scotch whisky. The response I received was brief and to the point:
"We have your letter about making films. If you wish to discuss this matter please telephone the undersigned to make an appointment." It was the most I could hope at that point for so I called to fix a date.

When I arrived at the company's office a week later I walked into a building which had changed very little in the last fifty years. Priceless paintings hung on the walls and the staff in reception spoke in hushed tones as if they were in church. I explained that I had come to see their advertising manager and was told to proceed to the third floor. One of the oldest lifts I have ever encountered got me to the right point and I knocked timidly at a highly polished door.

"Come!" a voice roared from within. I entered to see a man in his mid-fifties sitting behind a very tidy desk in a room which could have been an exhibit in a Scottish museum The company's advertising boss stood up to greet me.

On first acquaintance, to a young and inexperienced soul like me, he was an intimidating sight. He had served with distinction in the war and knew what being in command was all about. He wasted no time and came straight to the point:

"You wrote to us about making films. I can tell you now there is no point in doing that. We have been making films for years and are quite happy with our present arrangements."

For once I was lost for words. I had pinned great hopes on the outcome of this meeting and now they had been dashed with his opening words. Should I get up and leave, or was it worth trying to extend what so far had been a very brief encounter. I decided to play for time.

"I know you have done wonderful things," I murmured, "but I thought you might be interested in some new

ideas".
He took off his glasses and leaned across the desk.
" Have you any idea how long this company has been trading?" he enquired.
"A very long time I should imagine," I replied, desperately wishing I knew the correct answer.
"Over a hundred and fifty years, and in that time let me tell you we have learned a thing or two! What makes you think you could do any better?"
It seemed my case was lost. I could see the films I had envisaged making vanishing in a mist before my eyes but I decided to persist.
"Even the best companies need new ideas from time to time," I suggested expecting to be shown the door. There was a very long pause and then he replied.
"If you really think you can come up with something which is good enough for us you are welcome to try, but I must warn you now. It is very unlikely you ever will. You can put any ideas you may have on paper, and send them to me. I promise you will get a very prompt response." And that was how our meeting ended. I had arrived with high hopes and left feeling totally dejected.
It took me a couple of hours to get over my disappointment and concentrate on what I eventually realised was just another challenge. The door was not shut. It was still ajar. If I could come up with a good idea there was still a chance that my initial optimism might be justified. The problem was going to be finding anything which would be good enough to change the status quo.
I decided to go for a long walk and rack my brains and started to stroll along the banks of the Thames.
My route took me past the National Film Theatre where they were showing a series of early silent films. Some very old photographs were displayed outside. One picture showed a girl tied to a railway line with a steam train approaching. That picture gave me the inspiration I required. I decided to put forward a plan to remake that

film in colour with a couple of important changes to the original plot. I would give the girl a shopping basket which contained a bottle of whisky. I would also introduce an extra character - a man in a veteran car. He would see the girl was in trouble and rush in to rescue her. At the last moment he would release the bonds which tied her to the track, steal the whisky in her bag and race away down the line. The picture would then fade out and the whisky company's name would then be superimposed.

I spent several days developing my ideas and then put them on paper, sent them off and sat back and waited. For a week there was no response then, when I was almost convinced that everything was lost, my telephone rang and I was asked if I would call to round to discuss my ideas the following day at 9 o'clock.

When I arrived I was greeted with a smile which came as quite a shock. My potential client pointed out that their advertising films needed to run for not more than sixty seconds. They were normally produced in several different versions. There would be an all-white cast version and the scenes would then normally shot again with a mixed race cast for Spanish and African territories. They would also need to be dubbed in a number of languages. As the idea I had proposed did not involve any dialogue, I knew it could be produced more economically. As it was basically a period scene, I thought it could probably be made with one cast in period dress, without any changes or additional costs. The figures began to add up and eventually the company decided to go ahead and that is when the going got tough. When clients approve a script they sometimes want it to be produced very quickly and that is what transpired on this occasion. A contract was signed and in a very short time I then had to find an old steam train and a railway line where we could stop the train for hours without disrupting normal services. I also needed a veteran car.

The driver of the car, and the girl we intended to tie to the railway track both had to be found and fitted for period costumes. The railway needed to have a road running alongside so the car could race with the train in the opening shot and screech to a halt at a suitable point. The hero could then rescue the lady on the track (and take her whisky).

Finding a road and railway which run side-by-side is difficult enough but this road had to look as if it was as old as the car. It could not be made of modern materials. I also had to ensure that there weren't any modern buildings, vehicles, TV aerials or people in contemporary dress, anywhere in sight. It was a challenging task and I spent the next two weeks travelling far and wide.

I eventually found the railway in Sussex. A small band of enthusiasts was in the process of setting up a railway preservation society. They agreed to help and my film became one of the first to be shot on what has since become a Mecca for movie moguls - The Bluebell Railway. Finding a veteran car took longer still. I contacted the Veteran Car Club and they gave me the names of a number of people who they felt might be able to help or advise. I telephoned the first name on the list. The man who answered was very deaf and it took several minutes to explain who I was and what I was looking for. After an exasperating call, in which he told me three times that he had recently been in hospital but failed to say anything about his car, I decided to go and see him.

The owner of the car was born around the year that it was built. It was a 1905 Renault. He was a lovely man with a passion for restoring old vehicles. Unfortunately he had reached an age where, like the vehicles he restored, everything did not always function as well as it should. His sight was failing and he could only hear one word in ten, but his enthusiasm was undiminished.

"Come for a ride," he said "then you will see what it is

all about." I watched as he reversed a sixty- year- old car out of his garage and then I climbed up and sat on the front seat beside him. The garage backed directly on to a main road which was always very busy. Ignoring the traffic my host drove into the middle of the road. Cars and lorries hooted and swerved to avoid us but my host did not hear. He continued to drive on and started to tell me all the gory details of his hospital visits. For ten minutes we missed death by inches time after time. When we eventually got back to his garage we parted as good friends but it took me the rest of the day and several large gins to calm my nerves.

I eventually found a Model T Ford and a driver who had been involved in making films before and in due course we assembled on location. The finished film would run for sixty seconds but I thought it would take us two days to shoot. There were so many things which might go wrong, and most of them did, as I mentioned at the beginning of this book. The weather was the first disaster. It poured with rain from the moment we arrived and the weather forecast promised conditions would remain unchanged. Train, car and cast took up their positions and we started to shoot. I have already described what happened then in the chapter one. We went on shooting for two days in arctic conditions. When everyone had been soaked to the skin several times, we managed to finish our last shot. It was a very difficult job but I am happy to report that the resulting film was a great success.

As word got around the fledgling business continued to grow. There is an old saying the movie world that you are only as good as your last picture and there seem to be some truth in that. If you make a stinker which fails to take off your phone will not ring and no one will want to know. Fortunately I have generally been lucky. As orders have come in I have and built up a team of people who know what they are doing and are pleasant to work with and it has gone on from there.

Our success in promoting whisky won us a commission to make a series of films for a major Dutch brewer. Heineken had long been a successful family run business but in the 1960s it was rapidly expanding and becoming an international brand. In Britain another family brewing business -Whitbread - signed an agreement to sell Heineken in the UK and built a brewery at Luton just outside London to make their beer under licence. Dutch brewers were imported to supervise the process and the raw materials used and recipes followed were said to be the same as those used in Holland. The resulting brew was excellent but people who knew the original Heineken taste felt it was never quite the same. I asked the people who set up the new brewery if that view was correct. I was told that there was only one ingredient which could not be imported economically and that was water. The Luton brew was made with a local supply, I later discovered that when the Irish brewer Guinness opened a brewery in London they had encountered a similar problem. Years later the London operation was shut down and all the Guinness drunk in the UK was imported from Dublin.

To get some publicity for their rapidly expanding brand' Heineken and Whitbread decided to make a number of films to be shown in cinemas and other places where audiences of young beer drinkers could be encouraged to drink the brand. We were commissioned to produce those films. Many had sporting themes and making them we got involved in a number of unexpected and sometimes bizarre events.

The first film to take off (quite literally!) told the story of the building and maiden flight of the world's largest hot air balloon. Today ballooning is a popular international sport but in the 1960's it did not attract much comment. It wasn't exactly new. The first man-made balloon took to the air in 1783 when two French brothers - Etienne and

Josef Montgolier flew in hand made balloon which was heated by burning straw. They managed to stay in the air for eight minutes proving that at last man could fly but it remained a very hazardous business.

Experiments continued using hydrogen and hot air and in 1863 a group of pioneers built a doubled deck balloon to carry eleven passengers in a two tier basket. It took off and crashed on its first flight, killing everyone on board. The balloon we were to film was based on the same Concept.

The Gerald. A Heineken as our balloon was named, was designed by Don Cameron - a young systems analyst who gave up a promising career in the aerospace industry to start a company making hot air balloons. He set up shop in a disused school in Bristol and went on to become a huge commercial success and one of the great adventurers of our age.

The balloon he planned to build would be the largest anyone had ever made. It would stand ten times taller than a London bus and hold half a million cubic feet of hot air heated by propane burners. Fifteen people would fly in a wicker basket which would be suspended underneath. The whole thing took six months to build. Three thousand yards of specially toughened fabric had to be measured, cut and stitched together. The basket was made by hand in a Bristol workshop for the blind. As work progressed we filmed every stage.

A trial inflation was made in a giant aircraft hangar near Bedford. It had originally been used for airships before the R101 crashed and ended interest in that way of flying for quite a long time. In controlled conditions the balloon inflated, rose eight feet and hit the roof as there as no more room but what would happen in the open air? No one knew but we were soon to find out.

On a wintry day in a field near Bristol 30 passengers and crew assembled in a deserted field near Bristol. Don was in excellent form and the brewery's public relations firm was encouraging everyone to enjoy what they assured us was going to be an historic event. They were eager and optimistic but before we were allowed to climb aboard we had to sign a disclaimer absolving the sponsors from any claims for damages if things went wrong.

We boarded and waited to experience the results of six months work.

The giant rose majestically into the air and, much to our relief, quickly reached a sustainable height where it remained level and stable. I, like most people, had never flown in a balloon before but any nervousness I had felt soon disappeared. The whole experience was delightful. For half an hour we drifted above the treetops and covered several miles in a gentle breeze. The hectic pace of everyday life seemed a long way away. We were up and away but the in due course it dawned on us that we still had to get down and land in one piece. Computer predictions has confirmed that the balloon should fly but on the subject of landing forecasts had proved harder to interpret. There were so many variable which had to be considered.

Gradually we began to lose height as Don and his co-pilot made coordinated moves reducing the heat applied by the balloon's hot air burners. As the heat decreased so did our height and the earth got nearer and nearer. |As our descent continued at an ever increasing pace we drifted towards a firm house and I envisaged us all crashing on the roof but our pilots skilfully steered us away, We landed with a bump at a speed which dragged the basket across a ploughed field for a hundred yards. The maiden flight of the world's largest hot air balloon had been an outstanding success.

The maiden fight was great but for us it was not the end of the story. Our work went on.

The film we had shot had to be edited. A commentary adding interesting facts which supported the pictures had to be written and recorded and then finished film could be

released.
I edited the pictures and wrote the words for a commentary which the sponsors wanted to be spoken by by Victor Borge, who was starring in the company's commercials at that time. Victor was a big international star and consequently a very busy man. I called his agent to arrange a recording time. He suggested I should discuss it with Victor himself. I eventually managed to contact him in New York where he had just arrived after completing a European tour. His diary was the kind of nightmare any big star is used to and it soon became clear that any prospect of his travelling to London to record anything in the next three months was going to be out of the question. He told me that he had just arrived in New York where he would be spending the week doing a series of live performances on stage which would also be broadcast live coast to coast across the USA. He suggested that I should meet him in Philadelphia the following week. We could then record our film in between his live stage shows. It seemed to be the best solution from both our points of view so I flew to the USA the following week.
Borge's show was being staged in a huge theatre owned by a national television network. I had flown in via New York and arrived in the early hours of the morning (UK time) just as his show was ending. Two thousand people had attended the show and millions more had watched it on television. I had not worked with Victor before and looked forward to working with him. We were both tired but we got on well and had numerous cups of coffee to keep us awake as we worked on the script.
I had brought the film to show him but in the early hours of the morning the projectionist had gone home so I had to try to describe what audiences would be looking at at each point. Fortunately Victor was an experienced star performer who quickly understood what was needed. We spent an hour on the script and then sat alone on the stage

of the 2000 seat theatre and recorded his words on a portable tape recorder. After a quick playback to ensure that everything was correct I took a cab to the airport and boarded the next flight to London. The film was released the following week.

Our association with Heineken continued for several years. Six months after *BALLOON* was released I found myself in Amsterdam once again once again. On that occasion we had been commissioned to film a rally of boats from the UK to Amsterdam. It was quite a big job with around a hundred boats taking part. The plan was that the boats would sail from Ramsgate and hopefully arrive in convoy at the centre of Amsterdam the following day. I planned to film the arrival with three cameras shooting simultaneously from different viewpoints. One would be stationed on roof of the harbour building which stands alongside Amsterdam's central station and commands superb views across the harbour. A second would be on board one of the boats taking part in the rally. For my third camera position I decided to charter a small aircraft which could fly slowly above the boats as they arrived in the harbour. The day before the boats were due to arrive, I went to Schiphol airport to charter a plane and arrange for its passenger door to be held open and pinned back so my cameraman could film through the open space and get an uninterrupted view. Engineers coped with my request and I thought no more about it until the following day when the event took place.

I stood on the roof of the harbour building on a beautiful summer day. The boats arrived in the harbour at the predicted time and we started to film. As the first boats reached the middle of the harbour the aircraft I had chartered appeared on the horizon and flew directly overhead. It was a spectacular scene and I felt confident that the cameraman on board would be doing justice to it. For a few seconds I took my eyes off the view and wrote a note about the shot we were recording. As I looked up there was a flash in the sky. My chartered aircraft made a very steep turn, lost height and sped away. I could not be sure what I had seen but I had a ghastly feeling that something might have fallen out of the plane and into the harbour. Could it have been my cameraman? Had his safety harness worked loose and allowed him to slip and fall several hundred feet in the water? The aircraft was now nowhere to be seen. I tried to contact my cameraman on a short wave radio but could not get through. Fearing a disaster I started to pray.

My worries continued until later that night when the cameraman who eventually returned and told me what had happened.

As he had started to shoot the plane had tilted slightly. A loose piece of wood, which one had noticed, slid across the floor and out of the aircraft's open door. As it fell out it had apparently hit the wing and set off an alarm which automatically alerted the nearest airport. That happened to be Schiphol - one of the busiest in Europe. Fortunately everyone had remained calm. The aircraft landed without any damage and the film was completed within the original budget and on schedule.

The Amsterdam harbour incident was not the last near disaster I was to encounter while filming in Europe.

The most serious occurred after I had been filming in Greece.

I had been shooting in Crete. When filming was competed I decided to travel back to Athens by boat and then fly home. I duly boarded one of the local car ferries. Like many Greek ships at that time it was fairly old and it ran every day between Pireus and Crete. The sea was rough and I remember the ship because it rolled so badly I was very sick. When I got off in Athens I was glad be on dry land again and set off for the airport to board a flight to London.

Back at base I concentrated on editing the film I had shot in and in a few days had almost forgotten about my most recent journey. On my way home I decided to buy an evening paper and catch up on any news I might have missed. The lead story was all about a Greek ferry. It was the Heraklion - the boat I had travelled on a few days before. The report described how she had sailed into a storm. A refrigerated lorry had broken loose and slammed into one of the side doors on the car loading deck allowing water to pour in. The ship had then capsized. There were 47 survivors and 241 people lost their lives.

Most of our travels for the rest of that year were within the UK. We spent a lot of time on farms shooting a number of quite interesting projects. We made several films for a north of England tractor company. Their publicity man - a down-to-earth Yorkshireman - was a joy to work with. Once we had managed to convince him that we knew what he wanted, he let us get on with our work and reserved judgment until he saw the finished film. He had done his job for years and knew more about the agriculture and the tractor industry than anyone I have ever met.The factory was vast. For years it had enjoyed considerable success and employed hundreds of people from miles around. At the height of its success the company decided to take over a huge conference centre in the south of France and invite important customers to fly in from all over the world to attend a special presentation. They asked me to write and produce that show. It was a huge undertaking and one that proved to be enjoyable and rewarding for all concerned.

My brief was to introduce a new range of tractors in a way which the very high powered audience would find interesting and entertaining. Having attended many thoroughly boring conventions myself I knew what to avoid and spent a lot of time trying to devise a format that which I felt would work. The presentation was eventually built round a stage show which I wrote so it would appear as it everything was going wrong while in fact it was proceeding exactly as planned. I wanted a very

English star to anchor the show and managed to persuade Brian Johnson to take time off from doing his celebrated test match cricket commentaries and make his first ever appearance centre stage as the star of our show. At first he was reluctant. His cricket commentaries had made him world famous and I knew audiences would like him and find any message he delivered to be entirely credible. At first he had doubts about working live on a stage in such a large venue. We discussed various ideas and eventually he agreed to give it a go. When the show took place he was ably supported by another hugely talented British actor - Derek Benfield who at that time was starring in a long running BBC drama series called THE BROTHERS. Together they made the show a roaring success. Even today people still talk about it as an event which broke new ground in making conference presentations a pleasure to watch.

Over the years we made films for several tractor companies but my personal favourite was always the one we had worked for first of all. We travelled to Yorkshire to make films for them any times and then we began to hear rumours that the were going to be taken over by a big American competitor. The rumours proved to be correct.

I arrived for one of my regular meetings with our contacts to find that they had suddenly been retired and a much younger American marketing executive had been appointed. He tried to do things in Yorkshire exactly as he had always done them in the USA. His letters were modestly signed with his name and position as a President Elect - Europe, Asia and the Middle East- a big a task for anyone and one for which he seemed to me to be totally unqualified. After the quiet efficiency of his predecessor, who knew everyone and was universally liked, it was a sad change. Sales began to drop and it was easy to see that problems lay ahead.

At the invitation of the new regime I attended one of

their international sales meetings, which they held in Paris. The American vice president spent several hours telling the heads of his European companies how they should be doing jobs which they had already done, with great success, for years. He knew almost nothing about Europe and ignored the differences in national culture and in the tractor market. Two years after that meeting the English factory closed and the entire staff, some with over thirty years' service, were made redundant. A well equipped modern factory was written off and orders were passed to factories in Germany and France, where the company's market share was also declining. It was a sad end to the careers of many talented people and a salutary lesson about what can happen when large American companies attempt to do business in Europe without enough research, and with the wrong people in charge. With the tractor factory closure we lost one of our first big accounts. Fortunately one of their competitors, who was familiar with our work, asked us to make films for them and we continued to do so for many years until they too were taken over. Then the same disasters happened again. An American parent company soon moved most of the company's production elsewhere. A foundry was closed down and a factory was reduced to assembling parts, which were largely produced in the USA. Again we lost a valuable contract but Britain's manufacturing industry lost very much more.

One of the great joys of working in film and television is that every job you are involved in is different. You may work one week on a film about tractors and a few days later be promoting the sales of whisky, holidays or almost anything else you care to mention. It is difficult to get bored and one quickly becomes a mine of information on a host of potentially very boring subjects. I am sure you have seen films which failed to excite you. At one time or another we have all had to sit through productions we would prefer to forget. Educational and documentary films can be particularly tedious and that is one of the things I like about the areas I chose to work in. At first sight many of the subjects I have been asked to film have seemed extremely boring. Making dull subjects interesting to watch is a challenge and it is one I have always found is difficult to resist.

After weeks filming in the open air on farms, we moved to one of the most enclosed locations I have ever had to film in. The British Nuclear Fuels reprocessing plant at Sellafied in Cumbria is a one-off location. There is nowhere else like it and, having filmed there on several occasions, I cannot claim to be too upset by that.

The nuclear fuel industry is very sensitive about its image and every year thousands of pounds are spent trying to ensure that the message the industry wants to be heard is put across. We won a contract to handle a small part of that massive task and made a film for showing to schools. In preparing the script I learned all about the advantages of nuclear power over traditional fossil fuels. I gradually found I was beginning to accept the view which the industry has promoted for many years. - that nuclear power is perfectly safe. If you have never set foot in the innermost working of a nuclear fuel plant, you may not be aware that its massive walls are built with very thick concrete. Double doors separate each area and you have to put on special clothing to pass inside. Between each set of doors, geiger counters are used to ensure your radiation level has not passed above accepted safety limits. It is all quite daunting but in a way it is also reassuring to see that so many safety precautions are being observed. From a filming point of view it is a nightmare. With clothing changes and radiation checks it takes ages to get from shot to shot. A simple scene can take days to film. It is also strangely depressing. With gray concrete walls and the constant sound of geiger counters monitoring every breath of air, it is not a particularly joyful place. We worked on undaunted,

and made an interesting little film. Shortly after it was completed there was an incident in a small Russian town which directly contradicted many of the points made in our script. As far as I am aware it has never been shown.
The name of the town was Chernobyl.

My mother and father

George & Mary - The brother and sister I never knew who died shortly After these pictures were taken.

Artist John Hutton at work in his studio.
This was my first independent production. It was eventually bought by the BBC and was one of the first programmes ever shown on BBC 2

Milton Abbey School as it is today and after the fire which destroyed the west wing in 1956

**Filming THE AFRICAN QUEEN
In Guernsey harbour**

The boat was originally featured in the classic Humphrey Bogart film.

It was derelict for years until it was found and restored by new owner who is the man you see here.

Shooting our first commercial on the Bluebell Line

Editing and dubbing DOCTOR WHO

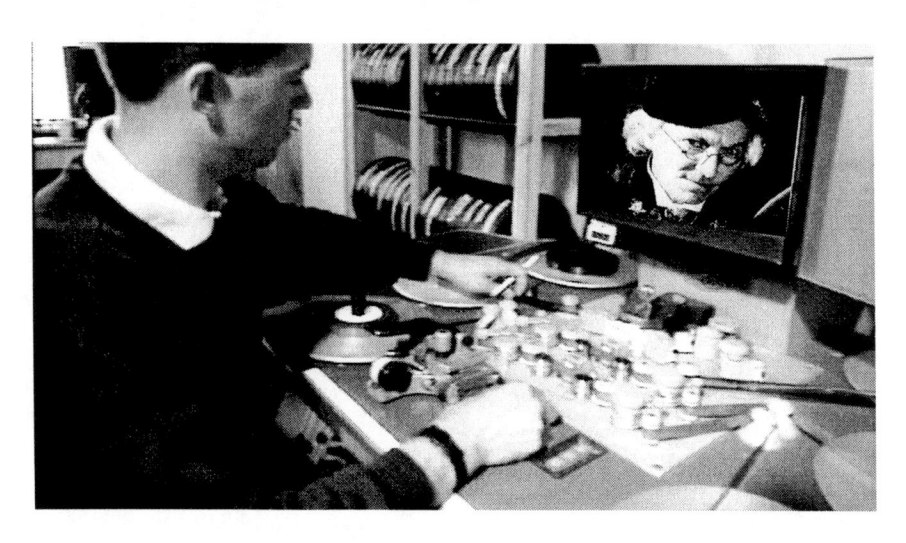

Top television cricket commentator Brian Johnson broke new ground in his career when he hosted a live presentation which we staged In Monte Carlo for an international audience

The world champion pie eater provided an a interesting opening for a film on medical records.

Filming DRINK & DRIVE?

With my assistant and friend John Ballard and a little help from a friendly pirate on a Royal Caribbean cruise ship

The QE2's captain welcomes the author

At Ealing Studios as a BBC trainee

On location in Sri Lanka. One of the many countries we have filmed in over the years.

Tommy Steele started his career as a ship's steward

We filmed him at his home when he was at the height of his fame and a big international star.

Fiming David Niven at his home in Cap Ferrat

Peter Ustinov drives his unique Hispano Suiza car. It was stolen shortly after this scene was

Filming Vincent Price in the Royal Pavilion Brighton when he was at the peak of his career as the king of horror movies.

Live television production
A studio gallery (top picture)
Part of a studio set (below)

Before videotape & DVDs
were invented everything was
shot on film which had to be
Processed & printed before
it could be edited and shown

5 – BEHIND THE SCENES

When you sit at home and watch television or go to a cinema, I hope you usually manage to enjoy whatever it is you have decided to watch. If you knew how much effort has gone into preparing it, you might appreciate it even more.

There are some who seem to believe that making a film or a television programme simply involves getting a few people together, pointing a camera in the right direction, taking a few shots and then cutting out the bad bits. If only that were true! Next time you start to watch whatever it is you have chosen to see, you may find it more interesting if you have some idea of what may have happened "off camera," when the epic you are viewing was being made. So let me take you behind the scenes and show you what you will probably not see in the finished picture.

As I write these words, I am sitting on the balcony of a seafront flat in Brighton. There is a busy road in front of me and beyond that the sea is shimmering in the morning sunlight. The flat is part of a regency terrace in what is normally a quiet part of this delightful seaside town. I have come here for a few days to escape from the pressures of my London office but the view from the balcony suggests I may have chosen the wrong time to arrive. A warning was issued several weeks ago, but I had forgotten all about it. It was in the form of a letter advising residents that on certain dates the area would be visited by a film company shooting scenes for a feature film. It is going to be a remake of a picture originally released in the 1940s. The letter told us when filming would take place and ended with a promise that those involved would endeavour to cause as little inconvenience as possible. It was the sort of letter I have often had to write myself, so it did not concern me very much when I found myself on the receiving end for a change.

I dismissed the subject from my mind and forgot all about it until I arrived today. Now the events referred to in that letter are about to take place, so come and join me on the balcony and I will tell you what is going on. I will also try to give you some idea of what it all means from a film maker's viewpoint and tell you what you will and will not see, if you happen to watch the finished film.

The film is set in England in the 1940s, after the end of the second world war. In the last few days, before the main body of film makers arrived, our street has been subtly transformed. A large apartment building a few doors away now bears a gold sign telling us it is The Grand Hotel. As it is clearly not intended to be quite as grand as the name suggests, the studio art department have painted rust patches on the sign and daubed some damp patches on the outside walls. They have also erected a pseudo iron portico, which looks quite impressive. It too has been toned down so the general impression is that this fictitious hotel has seen better times. On the seafront a modern bus shelter has been disguised by putting up a false wall and a few 1940 advertising signs. All modern fencing has been removed and the double yellow lines on the main road have been obscured so now there is nothing modern in sight. It has been done quickly and with some style. It looks just right for the period they are trying to re-create and whoever is designing this particular film is clearly very good at his or her job.

Now the first technicians and actors are beginning to arrive. It's a mini invasion. The catering wagons were first on the scene. It seems they are preparing to feed an army. Generator vans and lorries filled with lights arrived at dawn and from then on the procession has continued. Now there must be around a hundred people in the area, all employed to shoot a few brief shots.

In trailers parked up the road, the main actors and a host of extras are putting on 1940s clothes. In other vehicles make-up artistes are changing faces to look right on camera. A few yards from my window, around twenty people are setting up the sound recording gear and two large Panavision cameras. Each camera has to be removed from the series of cases in which it is stored and then, assembled, checked and mounted on a wheeled camera dolly.

In the two hours since dawn, the view from my window has been completely transformed. All modern cars, except those roaring past on the busy seafront road, have miraculously disappeared. Three pre-war cars are now parked near the newly created Grand Hotel, waiting for orders to move into action. A policeman and a host of assistant directors, all linked by two-way radios, have moved into carefully planned positions to ensure that when the cameras roll, nothing modern will be allowed to spoil the scene. When the director calls for action, the flow of traffic will be stopped. The three vintage cars will then drive at a predetermined distance and speed past the area where the

main action is to going take place. On the director's cue actors will then walk out of the hotel. A camera will track back with them as they move across the main road towards the promenade where they will stop and look out to sea.

From the camera's viewpoint, everything will appear to be happening in the late 1940's. It's a simple enough shot but getting everything to happen in the right way at the correct moment requires a huge amount of planning and organisation. Even in an apparently straightforward scene like this, there are so many things which can go wrong. In this instance, as I watch I can see that this production is in the hands of an excellent team. They have done their homework and they deserve to succeed, but unfortunately in any situation like this, success does not entirely depend on the film makers. As cameras roll, there are so many things which can make a "take" unusable. Artistes may forget their lines or deliver them in a way, which the director does not like. The wardrobe department may have accidentally failed to observe that one of the actors is wearing a modern digital watch – a prop which would look quite out of place in a movie supposed to be set in the 1940's. Aircraft may pass overhead, spoiling the sound, or the camera may move too far or at the wrong speed, losing focus showing things which need to be out of shot. Rehearsals and an experienced production team can eliminate most of these problems but there are things which even the best crew cannot always be expected to anticipate.

From my balcony, which is just out of shot, I can see that they are now almost ready to shoot the first scene of the day. It will not be the first shot in the finished film. They have already filmed at other locations and in a studio for several weeks. The actors will have to pick up the threads and ensure their performances today will work when they are cut onto scenes which have already been shot. Now they seem to be ready to go. The police have stopped all the modern traffic on the seafront road at a point fifty yards from where the action will take place. On a cue from the director, the vintage cars are now making their manoeuvres. The hotel door opens and the two leading artistes appear and start their short walk. I can see the camera moving backwards, a few yards ahead of them. The view audiences will see simply shows two people, walking from the rather faded Grand Hotel, past a few cars. They are holding what looks like a fairly intimate discussion. Observant audiences may notice that in the background a hotel porter is helping some other people to move some luggage. It's a lovely sunny morning but just below the camera technicians are feeding a steady stream of smoke (produced by dry ice) to lend atmosphere to the scene and make it look as if it is a cold and rather misty autumn day.

What the actors are seeing at this time is different again.

In their minds they have to be in character, physically becoming the two people they are supposed to be. They have to remember their lines and moves, which have been worked out to very precise parameters during rehearsals. They must ignore the camera, the smoke gun and small army of people who are walking backwards behind the camera as they approach the promenade. They must also forget that 50 yards away there is now a queue of modern cars waiting to be allowed to drive along the road they are now using. Together they are all creating an illusion and it has to look and sound right. The scene lasts less than a minute then the director calls "cut!" The police allow traffic to flow again and those involved in shooting the scene pause to discuss the results of their work. It is soon clear that they are not happy and they move back to their starting points. The camera is checked. Make-up is re-examined and all the fine points which have to be considered before the camera rolls are run over once again.

Fifteen minutes later everyone is ready for another take. Take two is announced. The traffic is stopped and the action begins again. From my viewpoint it all looks fine but I am not seeing what the director and the cameraman are trying to convey. As the actors reach the promenade, the action is stopped again. Something has gone wrong. What it could be this time? Perhaps tiny specks of dust have collected in the camera, spoiling the carefully framed image or damaging the film. Or maybe an overhead microphone, which should not be seen, has dropped too low and appeared in shot. Or did one of the actors get a word or a sentence wrong or miss one of those chalk marks on the road, which have been put there to remind the cameraman of a particular focus point? There are so many things to consider in the quest for perfection.

Now it's back to the start again. Take three appeared to be going without a hitch, until one of the motorists the police have stopped got fed up with waiting, sounded his horn and started shouting from his car. That ruined the sound so it all had to be done again. On the next take an aircraft flew directly overhead, spoiling the sound again and on the fifth take a holidaymaker ignored the cordoned-off area and walked into the camera's view on the edge of the scene. And so it went on, until eventually perfection was achieved and at last everyone was happy. The situations I have described may sound strange but to anyone who works in films what has happened here this morning is all perfectly normal. It always takes time. Today around six hours have so far been spent on what will probably end up as around one a minute of finished screen time. Before filming began at all, months of work had to be done getting the script right and negotiating contracts for all the artistes and extras. Costumes had to be designed, made and fitted, and a detailed shooting schedule had to be prepared. It had to take into account the actors' other commitments and those of the key technicians who needed to be involved .Every location had to be chosen, checked and adapted to meet the needs of the script. Before the scenes I have just described could be filmed, there must have been many meetings with the police and local authorities to get agreement to stop the traffic and move modern items out of view. And when filming is completed there will still be much work to do. Editing is one of the most important stages in any film's production. Scenes have to be assembled in the right order, because very few films are shot in the order in which the scenes will eventually occur. Every shot has to be cut at precisely the right point to make the action interesting to watch. A final soundtrack must then be prepared combining location recordings with music, sound effects and possibly new dialogue, recorded to replace any made unusable by disturbances on location. It can take months and sometimes years. Even a simple film will often take weeks if not months to plan and get together. It's a daunting task. So next time you watch a film or a TV programme, spare a thought for the people who made it. Making movies is not quite as simple as it may at first sound!

In most jobs patience is an asset. In the film business it is essential. Working with a large film unit, like the one I have just described, you have extensive resources on call and usually a good support team back at your production office. I have enjoyed working like that for years, but when I first started to run my own production company it was a different story. Film companies come and go. I believe the average life from formation to bankruptcy is around three years. We have so far managed to survive for over 40 years. Don't ask me why or how. I just don't know! Luck must have played a major part. In the early days it may also have been because we decided to make the sort of films people were prepared to pay us to produce. They were not necessarily the films we wanted to make. Every would-be film-maker, and many well established professionals, has pet subjects which he or she would love to film. One of the hard lessons one has to learn if one is to survive, is that those subjects are often either too expensive to make or of such a minority interest any investment in them would be unlikely to produce a decent return. I was lucky enough to realise that before I spent too much money. I concentrated on jobs which would bring is cash, and that took me to places and involved me in situations which relatively few people are ever likely to encounter.

As I have already mentioned, one of the nice things about working in films is that every day is different. One rarely has to do the same thing twice. Over the years I have found myself in some fairly strange situations. In the last few months I have stood alongside a surgeon doing a hip replacement operation and have dangled from a harness under a helicopter filming a power boat race. I have been driven round one of London's busiest squares on a fire engine at sixty miles and hour (on the wrong side of the road!) and have found out what would happen if the fuel caught fire on a jumbo jet. It makes life interesting, if you manage to survive!

Quite a lot of my time has been spent making what used to be known as public service films. That is the rather posh term given to the sort of mildly educational films we used to see at school. Like so many things in life, my involvement in that particular type of work came about by chance.

One day there was a fire in a flat a few doors away from where I was then living. The owner left a chip pan unattended while she went to answer the phone. In seconds the whole kitchen was alight. By the time the fire brigade arrived flames were shooting through the roof. It was frightening to see how much damage a simple mistake could cause in such a very short time. I had never seen anything like it before and it really made me think. I found myself wondering how many other people, like me, did not really appreciate how many problems could be caused by making such a simple mistake. Perhaps a film should be made to let them know? I felt it should and that was how I first got involved with public service films.

I knew what I wanted to do, and felt there would probably be a market if the film I envisaged was made in the right way. I also knew that it would be quite Expensive to produce and that money would have to be found to finance the production before any work could start. I eventually managed to persuade an insurance group to put up some cash and started to prepare what was to prove to be quite a successful venture.

You can make any educational or training film in a number of different ways. The boring way is to pay some "expert" to stand up and talk to camera and put the obvious message across. That sort of approach, which I personally loathe, is done far too often simply because It is cheap. It is much easier, and thus cheaper, to describe something instead of showing it. In our fire film for example, it would have been very easy to arrange for an experienced fire officer to deliver a lecture which we could film, inserting a few examples of what he was talking about from time to time. That would probably have got the message across, if anyone managed to stay awake watching it, but it was not what I wanted. Having had to sit through hours of boring educational films at school I have always tried to avoid inflicting the same punishment on anyone else. My mission has always been to try to make even the most boring subjects come to life. The fire film was the first occasion on which I was able to put that policy into practice.

When the money needed to finance a production has been arranged, the next move is to do some research. You have got to learn all about the subject you intend to film, especially if you are going to write the script. When you have researched as many subjects as I have over the years, you have to be very careful not to unwittingly become the ultimate party bore – a mine of useless information, who can rant on for hours on a range of totally boring subjects! Most subjects can be made interesting if you take the right approach. To do that, you sometimes have to go to great lengths to find things which will enliven what might otherwise fail to come to life. And that is where research comes in. As I knew almost nothing about fires, apart from the obvious fact that they were unpleasant and fairly common occurrences, I decided to start by getting some expert advice. I turned to the London Fire Brigade and spent several hours talking to fire officers and people working at fire stations in various parts of London. At that time there was a general interest in what I was proposing to do and a willingness to co-operate. The idea of a fire training film for the general public was then quite new and everyone wanted to help.

One of the officers I met suggested I should join him at

work on the night of November 5th. In England, that is always a big night for fire brigades because that is the date on which people remember Guy Fawkes – the man who tried to blow up the Houses of Parliament. Bonfire parties and firework displays are held all over Britain. Most are well organised and properly controlled but some inevitably get out of control. There is also evidence that arsonists sometimes choose this particular day to get in on the act. That night I met the senior fire officer who had invited me to join him in the central control room where fire emergency calls are received. As the evening progressed the incident board, which shows how many fires are being dealt with at that particular time, got busier and busier. The board shows where each fire is and indicates how many appliances are in attendance. In a heavily built up-area, or in a place where there are special risks like disabled people or large stocks of highly flammable materials, the initial attendance will usually be high. If a factory which is known to use potentially hazardous materials catches fire, more fire engines will be dispatched when the alarm is raised than will be sent if fire breaks out in a bungalow in the middle of field. When fire crews first reach the scene of a blaze, the senior officer present calls back to base to describe exactly what is happening. If he or she feels the blaze is too big to handle with the appliances which have been sent, a request will be made for that attendance to be increased.

"Make pumps five", is what you will hear if you happen to be eavesdropping, as I was on that occasion. When it gets to "make pumps ten," you know you have a serious fire.

For a couple of hours we stayed in the control room, watching the increasingly hectic activity as more and more calls came in. A wide range of different Emergencies was being handled with calm efficiency by all concerned. By nine o'clock it was clear that one

Particular blaze was in danger of getting out of control. Numerous appliances had been dispatched and requests for more were still coming in. My host, no doubt aware that the incident showed signs of getting nasty, headed for the door and I joined him. His specially equipped car was parked outside. In seconds we were moving at considerable speed through the busy streets of London. With siren sounding and blue lights flashing, my host drove with amazing skill through and round a series of obstacles. The speedometer crept up as other vehicles saw us approaching and moved out of the way. In a fraction of the time it would have taken in a taxi, we arrived at the scene of the blaze. It was an old warehouse quite near The Tower of London and by the time we arrived, five floors were already ablaze. Fire engines were parked in all directions and a well-organised operation was well underway.

When the fire brigade agreed to offer me their co-operation I had to sign a disclaimer form, absolving them from any claims for accident or injury. I signed without really thinking about what I might encounter. The warehouse fire made the dangers very clear indeed. Suitably protected, I moved with the fire crews towards the blaze. The battle was on to stop to prevent the fire spreading and save other properties nearby. We entered the burning building and for the first time in my life I came face to face with a wall of fire.

The sound the fire made was scary but as we moved inside it was the darkness, smoke and damp which immediately hit me. We were still some distance from the seat of the fire, but there was thick smoke everywhere. As water from firemen's hoses hit the walls it turned to steam. In a few seconds, I did not know where I was. When there is smoke all around, you quickly lose any sense of direction and it become difficult to breathe. Fortunately the fire officers I was with had made sure I did not stray. They knew what was going on and when

they suddenly turned and started to run, I followed them
without any second bidding. Minutes later the area we
had been in spontaneously exploded in a ball of fire.
What firemen call a flash-over had occurred.
Their experience and skill had ensured that
we had got out in time and no one was injured.
That fire was eventually contained and extinguished. It
taught me a lot and the knowledge I acquired proved
invaluable when I started to write a script.
The main thing I learned was that fires can spread incredibly
quickly. I had also failed to appreciate that the
biggest killer in any fire is smoke, not flames. I now
know why it pays to be prepared for any emergency and
to discover where your fire exits are. In a real emergency
there may not be time to find out.
I spent several more days with fire crews in different
parts of London. After the November 5th activity there
were no more major fires but I was certainly never bored.
There were plenty of interesting things to observe. Fire
crews have to answer a wide range of different calls and
on the days I spent riding on fire engines with a variety of
crews, I was able to witness at first hand a number of very
different incidents.
When I visited a West London fire station we sat around
for hours waiting for anything to occur. At last alarm
bells started to ring and crews ran to join a turntable
ladder and two fire appliances. I raced to join them. As
we drove out of the fire station I asked the driver what
kind of incident he had been called to. With two fire
engines and a turntable ladder I was anticipating quite a
big blaze. As we sped through the streets with sirens
sounding, scattering traffic in all directions, the driver
explained that we had been called to a tall block of flats
which had a garage and a petrol filling station underneath.
Someone living on the fifth floor had raised the alarm. I
had visions of flames shooting out of windows and petrol
exploding in the garage down below, while people slid

down sheets to save their lives. What we found when we arrived, proved to be a very different story.

As we drew up outside there were no obvious signs of a fire. The fire crews raced up to the fifth floor address which had been given when the emergency call was made. Down below two fire engines and a huge turntable ladder were prepared for action. I joined the senior fire officer as he ran up the stairs to the fifth floor. There was no smoke and no fire. Instead we found a nattily dressed young man who casually said "Ah there you are. About time too. I'd almost given up."

As we had just driven at breakneck speed through some of London's busiest streets and raced up five flights of stairs, it seemed a pretty odd response. The facts, which subsequently emerged were even stranger.

There wasn't any fire and there never had been. There wasn't any real emergency but the young man thought there was. He had been taking drugs all night and had been locked out of his flat by a jealous lover. In a fit of range he had called the Fire Brigade to help him to get back. Today the law has been changed, but at that time fire crews were obliged to answer every call they received. As the building was potentially a high-risk area, with many people living there and a garage down below, any call had to be answered with two appliances and a turntable ladder. It was an expensive fiasco. The firemen were incensed but grateful that, on this occasion, no lives had been at risk. Not surprisingly that incident did not make it into the script for our film!

The crews at that fire station dealt with several other calls that day. At lunchtime they were sent to another block of flats. On that occasion the wife of the man who raised the alarm had gone away. He had cooked lunch for himself and succeeded in frying a pork chop and his kitchen curtains.

One of the many lessons I have learned over the years is that, when you set out to make a film, you need to have one aim and a clearly defined target audience. If you try to do too many things in one film, you will probably fail to meet any of your objectives. You have to consider your aims, narrow them down and be quite specific. I knew I wanted to make a film alerting people to the dangers of fire, but the research I had carried out made me aware that my aim needed to be much more specific. Fires occur on all kinds of premises and they start in a lot of different ways. It would clearly be impossible to explore every aspect of such a vast subject in a fifteen minute film. My script would have to be selective and aim to get a limited number of points across to the sort of audiences it was being made for. Identifying those points called for research. The insurance company paying for the project wanted a training programme they could show to people who worked in factories, offices and other commercial premises. I read hundreds of insurance claims and reports into the causes of some very expensive fires. Several had been stared by electrical faults. Arson was another common cause. Arsonists often think their crimes will not be detected but with modern forensic techniques it is surprising how much evidence can be found even in a building which at first sight may appear to be totally destroyed. The reports I read included one on a fire n a large office block where a security man had set the place alight because he felt his efforts were not being appreciated. Then there was a factory where people were quite unaware that the solvents they had used for years to clean their machines were actually flammable because no one had ever told them. And there was another office block which was destroyed in a blaze which cost several million pounds. The evidence all suggested it had started in in a light fitting which everyone knew had been faulty for months. It had flickered on and off from time to time, but no one had thought it was worth reporting.

Those case histories, and thousands more, were all taken

into account and gradually the theme for our film emerged. *ALL ABOUT FIRE*, as the film was eventually called, showed how fires start and spread and how disasters can be prevented. It was deliberately designed to appeal to a wide audience – virtually anyone who works in commerce and industry. It was, and continues to be, a considerable success.

When shooting that film we scoured the country for firsthand examples of good and bad practice. We also staged a number of re-constructions. On one occasion we ourselves came near to disaster. We were shooting some shots in a small studio. I wanted to try to show how the vapour, which is given off by liquids like petrol, behaves. When you fill up your car, if conditions are right you can sometimes see vapour escaping from the filler point. A lot of people fail to realise how volatile that vapour is. There are also many who are unaware that inflammable vapours are given off by many other liquids. They may be labelled as "thinners" or "cleaning fluids," but they also produce vapour and if they are not treated with care it may start a fire.

I wanted to show how vapour can spread and arranged to film a small-scale demonstration. For a couple of hours we experimented with different types of lighting to get the effect we required. Eventually everything was ready for the camera to roll. We started to shoot and used a lighted taper to ignite a small amount of vapour, which we had funnelled through a cone. On the first take it lit just as we wanted but the lamps we were using proved to be too bright. We made adjustments and ran the camera again. As the taper came into shot, there was an explosion and a sudden flash of flame. The background scenery caught fire in seconds and before we could realise what was happening the whole room was ablaze. It was all very frightening. Fortunately, before we started shooting, we had for once decided to practice what we preached. We had placed powder fire extinguishers at each end of the set. It was the first time we had been wise enough to take such a precaution and it probably saved our lives. In a couple of minutes we managed to put out the blaze. The set was a write-off and the room could not be used for weeks, but we were all alive. Subsequent investigation showed that after the petrol had been poured for the first take, someone had forgotten to put the lid back on a container. Vapour had thus continued to escape. Quickly (but invisibly) it had filled the whole set. When it reached the flame, the vapour instantly exploded – graphically illustrating the very point which our demonstration had been designed to make. So, our audiences were not the only people who learned from that film. I have been extremely fire safety conscious ever since!

Several years after producing *ALL ABOUT FIRE* I was asked by a country fire brigade to make a documentary about their work. Cambridgeshire Fire and Rescue Service wanted to show people in their area what the fire service part of their council tax actually pays for. Having spent several weeks watching their activities from every point of view, I can assure them they are getting great value for their money. Until I was asked to make that film, I did not realise just how many different jobs a rural fire and emergency service is expected to do. If you do not live in the country, and have not had to be helped by one of the emergency services, you may find the things I discovered surprise you as much as they did me.

Dealing with fires is only part of the job. It's a pretty demanding part, and it takes around three years to become a qualified fire officer, with room for even more training in specialist skills and further advancement. I was once stupid enough to think that firemen only put out fires, but my experiences in Cambridgeshire soon put an end to that. In our film we covered a selection of the emergencies they had to attend. On the first day they had to rescue a horse which had fallen in a ditch. A few days later they worked through the night trying to prevent a blaze spreading through the thatched roof of an ancient pub. In the middle of that they had to cut a family out of a car which had been crushed in a motorway accident. They even found time to rescue a greedy, cat which got its head trapped in a tin of food! The most interesting part of the job was the attitude of the men and women involved in doing the work. They were very conscientious and they really cared. In this day and age I found that very refreshing.

Training is important in any job, but in the emergency services it is crucial. If you are not thoroughly competent you can lose your life or put others at risk. That fact was brought home to me quite early in our filming. We joined fire crews on a number of training exercises, and filmed them as they carried out a variety of tasks. We crawled through drains, filming young firemen being taught how to cope with poisonous gasses. The exercise we were filming was based on an incident which had occurred a few weeks earlier, when some children had started playing at one end of an old drain. With the natural curiosity of kids, they had managed to get inside and crawl along a maze of pipes. They soon found they were completely lost. On that occasion, someone heard them shouting and called for help and the firemen we filmed had been able to recall their training and prevent a disaster.

The second exercise we filmed involved a bus which appeared to have crashed and rolled down a hillside. It was a staged incident and no one was really hurt, but the old bus we used made it all seem quite realistic. We watched as basic first aid was applied to volunteer casualties. The carefully planned procedures, which can make the difference between life and death in a real emergency, were thoroughly tested as the cameras rolled.

Like all films, this one gave us a number of surprises. I was shocked to discover how much administrative work emergency services now have to cope with. There are endless committee meetings, politicians, regulations, and EEC directives whose combined efforts make quite difficult to do anything. There are reams of written instructions for everything. It is very difficult for fire brigades to even light a fire for training purposes. There are so many petty rules about health and safety. Most fire training now has to be done in specially constructed buildings where any smoke used can be strictly controlled. In a real emergency fire crews are still expected to perform miracles, and they often do. In training, their work is often hampered by petty rules and regulations and the bickering of small time officials who should know better. In spite of all that, the emergency services manage to cope and their performance is impressive as we tried to show in the film we produced.

If you are one of those people who are concerned about public service costs, you care to know that all the services of the fire brigade in that area cost the local taxpayers about the same as a pint of milk a week and if that is not a bargain I would like to know what is.

The success of *ALL ABOUT FIRE* prompted an approach from another insurance group. Their main interests were in road safety. You do not need to be a genius to realize that road accidents cost far too many lives and they occur every hour of every day.

Everyone who drives is potentially vulnerable - a point that was brought home to me very clearly when I was driving home from work on a November day.

I had just joined a motorway and suddenly found myself enveloped in very thick fog. One moment the sun was shining and then seconds later I could only see a few metres ahead. I adjusted my speed and started to pray. Fortunately at that point I was nearing the end of my journey and was able to turn off the motorway at the next junction.

The following day before I sent to work I turned on the television news. The lead story was a report on a accident involving forty lorries and cars which had run into each other in thick fog and the caught fire. It had happened a few miles from the point where I had left the motorway on the previous day.

That incident worried me for days and resolved to make the production of a road safety film my next priority. I approached various police forces for advice and help. At one place, which shall remain nameless, I was introduced to a chief superintendent who lost no time in telling me that he had always wanted to be in films and would be delighted to help with anything we required. The chief superintendent was very good at his job. The only trouble was that he had done it for so long he had got bored. His colleagues, who were well aware of the situation, were keen to make his talents available to anyone who would take him off their hands for a few hours. His eagerness to appear in front of the cameras and become a movie star was quite difficult to handle. Considerable tact was required. To me he was not really the right man to appear on camera. We wanted our film to appeal to young people and show things which would interest them. He wanted to stand up and explain what his experience of driving had taught him and why it paid to obey the law. I eventually managed to solve the problem by arranging to shoot a test. The chief superintendent was given a carefully prepared script and asked to speak a few sentences to camera. He was overjoyed at the prospect and looked forward to it for days.

When the camera started to roll, he suddenly found his lips were sealed. For the first time since we had met, he could not say a word. He was scared stiff and very upset. As tactfully as I could, I explained that we had met many other people who were brilliant at the jobs they had been trained to do but were not really cut out to appear "on camera." That was perfectly true. Just a few weeks before, a world expert on asbestos had been flown to

London from Australia to for us to film him. His flights and expenses had been paid by a company which was determined to record his views on film. We spent half a day trying to get him to talk and ended up with very few words. He managed " Hello – I am a doctor," and then he froze up. It is not everyone who can manage to talk to a camera with any degree of success.

Our police superintendent had another interest too – gin. My colleagues soon christened him the chief *sip*erintendent. Off camera he was very good at his job and the experience and knowledge he provided did much to ensure the film's ultimate success.

Public service films can easily be boring. We have all had to sit through well intentioned films which have been desperately dull to watch. As a film maker I have always tried very hard to make even the dullest subjects interesting and explore them in a way which will appeal to the audiences they are intended for. Young audiences in particular are easily bored and films made for them need quite a lot of thought.

When drinking and driving laws first came into force, I was asked to make a film for schools outlining the new laws and explaining why they had been introduced. The government department involved wanted a straightforward factual programme consisting of facts and figures with captions summarising the key points covered by the new laws. They offered to make a government minister available to introduce the film and say how important he felt it was. I was not very popular when I said that I felt that was not a good idea. Whilst I welcomed any support which any ministers might wish to give the film in subsequent interviews in the press, I felt that any establishment figure talking to camera and spouting lots of facts and figures would quickly alienate the young audiences we needed to be concerned with. I wanted to convince them that it was in their own interests not to drink and drive and not to simply tell them that they must not to do it. With that aim in mind and with the help of some colleagues I decided to arrange a test. With the advice of the police and the help of a university research scientist, we arranged to take over a disused miles from anywhere. We recruited a number of volunteers from local colleges and asked them if they would agree to take part in our tests. We then built an obstacle course, designed to test the judgment of drivers on a short test drive. As they drove round our course, the volunteers were asked a number of general knowledge questions. Their answers were recorded on tape machines which were fixed inside the cars they were driving. That was intended to simulate the effect of passengers talking to them, as they drove round the course. The proceedings were filmed by several cameras placed at strategic points round the course and by others inside the cars.

Before they drove at all, each driver was given a glass of what appeared to be an orange drink. Sometimes it was exactly that - pure undiluted orange. On other occasions the juice was mixed with vodka, in precisely measured amounts. Each driver was then asked to drive round the course twice – once twenty minutes after drinking and again an hour later.

On the day filming was due to take place, our volunteers were collected by bus and asked to sign consent forms, which included a promise that they would not drive again for at least 24 hours. In pouring rain the tests then began. We filmed all day. At the start of the Proceedings I must admit I was not sure what the results would prove. Like many young people (yes, I was also young then!) I had my doubts about all the propaganda being published in the media to discourage drinking and driving. Secretly I think I rather hoped that
the results would show the situation was not as serious as people made out.

It was a fascinating experiment. As alcohol levels rose the drivers reactions got slower and slower. They hit obstacles which they had managed to miss when they were sober. Reversing into a space which was about the size of the average garage proved to be the hardest task of all. A third of the competitors completely misjudged the length and width of their cars. As they got more confident with alcohol inside them, several drivers became quite aggressive. Their replies to the questions they were being asked got wilder and wilder. We were not administering very large doses of alcohol. Our drinks contained far less than most of our drivers would probably have consumed on a night in a pub but the results were indisputable. Without exception, no one drove well when he or she had had a drink, and some made a mess of the simplest manoeuvres.

Our tests proved convincing and interesting to watch, but I was still not satisfied.

I thought young audiences would want to know more before they would be convinced. With that in mind I went back to the police forces that had helped us to set up our tests. I showed them the results and gave them details of the blood alcohol levels of the drivers involved but did not reveal their true identities. The police were immediately interested in what our tests had revealed and were used to the reactions our drivers had shown as their blood alcohol levels had steadily increased. They had seen it all before in real life. As they watched the film they began to recall incidents they had seen where people had been injured or killed and alcohol was involved. I listened to their experiences and immediately knew what we must do if our film was going to help the young audiences we were concerned with. We had to find a way of bringing our carefully staged tests and the incidents the police had recalled together in an interesting and credible way and that was going to need more research.

I spent a month delving through transcripts of court cases and police accident reports. I studied hundreds if incidents where alcohol had been involved and in each instance found out what had actually happened and the blood alcohol levels recorded at the time by the officers involved. I wanted to find evidence of real life incidents where blood alcohol levels had been the same as those we encountered on our tests. I eventually found a number which matched. We then set out to show how those accidents had occurred and to reconstruct them. It was a slow process and a very unpleasant one, because in all accidents we re-constructed people had died. They included a university student who had an argument with his girl friend, got drunk and ended in a river. In another incident a young motorcyclist had misjudged his speed and collided with a car. The accidents we reconstructed had involved people from rich and poor families, all over Britain. There was only one thing they all had in common. Their lives, and the lives of the friends and families who survived them had effectively ended when those accidents occurred.

Making *DRINK AND DRIVE?* took several months of very hard work. It was withdrawn from circulation ten years after it was made because the cars featured in it were beginning to look dated but the message, and the results of the tests we had staged are as relevant today as they were when the film was made. It has since become something of a cult video which police forces and safety authorities still find is relevant today. As I write these words it is in digitally restored so it can be released again on DVD.

After the sobering experience of filming some of the grimmer aspects of road safety, I was commissioned to make an educational film on a much lighter
theme. This time the subject was to be the story of water, and the film was to be designed for showing in schools. We all take water for granted. It was only after spending some time in Saudi Arabia that I started to realise just how valuable it is. There water is more highly prized than petrol, and it is certainly not taken for granted on

any occasion. In the western world we think we know it all, and we don't always give water the attention it deserves. That was why the water company which approached me wanted to make a film. They wanted to show what their work involved and convince the public that every penny they invest in water is money well spent.
For two weeks I did everything I could to learn about water and the activities of the company which was Commissioning our film. I attended the opening of a new water treatment works, and witnessed the unveiling of a plaque by a totally complacent member of Parliament, who had held his seat for years and didn't care a damn. I then went on to study sewage which was much more fun because I found myself in the hands of a real enthusiast. To claim that Jack lived, slept and dreamed about sewage would perhaps be over the top, but his genuine love of the tasks he was responsible for brought tears to my eyes. They were tears of mirth, but fortunately he never realised that. Jack had started work in the local sewage plant as soon as he left school and he had been there for years. He had seen it all, but his enthusiasm for the processes he now managed was undiminished. As we toured the works, every dial, pond and pump was pointed out with glee.
"This is where it all starts," he announced as we began to tour the works. Everything arrives here. What the good people of the borough send us each day, and a good sprinkling of cuddly toys and false teeth." From then on I knew I was on to a winner!
We told Jack's story well and the film reflected his enthusiasm which made it a success. Over the years I have been involved in a number of other quite specialised projects. Shortly after the sewage experience, I found myself making a number of training films for doctors and surgeons. Our client was a firm which looks after the legal interests of doctors who are in trouble. It was, and still is, a first class organisation run by dedicated people

who are all extremely well qualified in their own particular fields which include dentistry, law and medicine.

I was fortunate in working with a man who had started his career as a young dentist, got bored and then qualified as a doctor. He then got bored again and studied law before eventually buying a farm and then drifting into semi-retirement. Dr Armond Gwynne was one of the most delightful people I have had the pleasure of working with. His knowledge was so great that it was difficult for an idiot like me to keep up with him. As the years passed we worked together on a number of very successful films. He knew law and medicine inside out, and I had a vague idea of what making films was all about. By pooling our resources, and not trying to do each other's jobs, we got results which seemed to work. Armond had gone through the mill of hospital training and practiced medicine for years in numerous environments. To him medical knowledge was an open book. As others were quick to point out, he actually knew a lot more than he would ever admit. He also had the rare knack of being able to impart that knowledge to other people.

The first film we made together was designed for audiences of surgeons. Its purpose was to remind them how surgical mistakes are sometimes made and to encourage them to follow the correct procedures. We wrote a script based on a number of real-life incidents. The names of the people involved, and certain facts, were altered for legal reasons. I seem to recall that part of the film dealt with a doctor who had accidentally amputated the wrong leg. In another scene we showed how a drunken lady with a head injury had been sent home without a full examination. He died the following day, and there were other situations which were relevant to any audience composed entirely of hospital doctors. Armond worked out the details of the cases. I then had to devise a way of linking them together in a script which the actors we intended to employ would be able to perform.

Doctors speak to their patients in fairly normal language, but when they talk to each other they sometimes use a lot of special terms. I knew that the dialogue I had to write must sound real to the surgeons who would watch our finished film. To do that, I realised I would have to use terms which they would feel were correct. With that requirement in mind, I arranged to join a surgeon for a day and watch him at work. I signed various forms, put on a surgical gown, mask and boots, and joined the surgeon and his team in an operating theatre. The first operation of the day was to be a hip replacement. I should tell you now that I have always been terrified of hospitals. For years I had vowed that I would never enter one as a patient, unless I was unconscious. You can thus imagine how surprised I was to find myself standing alongside a surgeon, with his scalpel poised. The sister in charge of the operating theatre later told me that she felt sure I would faint, and had already detailed a nurse to ensure I did not fall across the patient. In the event, the whole affair was clearly so routine and well organised that any fears I had once had completely disappeared. I found myself enthralled by the professionalism displayed by all the members of the team and was deeply reassured by what I saw. The only problem was that my visit proved to be useless for the purpose for which it had been arranged. I wanted to listen to the surgeon and his team, and note how they spoke as the operation progressed. In the event, they all knew their jobs so well that they failed to communicate on a single useful point. There was some conversation. The surgeon started it. As the patient's stomach was turned inside out, he calmly Asked his colleagues "Did you watch the cricket on Saturday?"

The anaesthetist checked that the patient was still breathing and then made his comments about the match.

The operation took about two hours to complete but the only knowledge I acquired was that England had played well after a poor start and had managed to win quite a good match!

In another medical film, which I made later with the same team, we were charged with the task of encouraging doctors to keep accurate medical records. Perhaps you think they do that already. On most occasions you are probably right, but our researches unearthed a number of problems which had been caused by doctors who had failed to ensure their patients' records were clear, accurate and up-to-date. There was one young doctor who wrote in his patient's notes, "This silly cow thinks she knows everything." It may have been true, but it did not sound good when she accused him of medical negligence and his notes were read out in court. Then there was the doctor whose writing was so bad a nurse misread a decimal point and injected a baby with a lethal dose. Incidents like those formed the basis of our script. They were examples of mistakes which are easily made, and ones which our training film was designed to prevent.

Making films for doctors, is certainly a challenge. They are not going to be impressed by flashing lights or shots of ambulances charging around with sirens blaring. Doctors are bright and they can see more of life in a week than many people do in a lifetime.

If you are write a script which states the obvious or talk down to your audience their attention will be lost from them from the very first shot. In our medical records film we tried, as always, to do something different. It was not the most exciting subject. Somehow it had to be brought to life. We needed a good opening scene. As I think I have mentioned before, the first few minutes of any film are crucial. You have got to grab your audiences' attention from the very first frame. If you begin with a boring scene, they will mentally switch off

and your fate will be sealed from that point on. So how would you start a film about medical records? It was quite a challenge!
Believe me, it is quite a challenge! I decided o use an unconventional idea hoping it would encourage audiences to look and listen to what was being said. The fist shot in the film showed a large tattooed man who was sitting at a table stripped to the waist. The camera moved back o so that on the tale there was a huge dish piled high with pork pies. The first sentences of the film's commentary explained that the man we were watching was the world pie eating champion. To win that title he ad managed to fifty pies in ten minutes. As we watched he started eating in an attempt to bet his own record. We held that scene for a few seconds and then showed a panel of judges who were seated nearby. They were very prim and proper and made a wonderful contrast with the burly man, who was pouring gravy on a rapidly diminishing stack of pies. The film's narrator quietly reminded us that the results of his record attempt would depend on the judge's assessment of his performance that day. They would make a note each time a pie was eaten. The important thing was the written record. It had to be accurate and complete for the man to stand a chance.
In a couple of minutes we had thus managed to introduce our theme – the subject of records. As the shots we used were entertaining we also managed to get audiences on our side. People started to watch and listen to what we had to say. It was then quite easy to switch to the importance of records in other settings. We moved to one which we knew our audiences would immediately recognise. It was a hospital ward. Another place where the accuracy of records is always crucial. The idea worked well and our film was very well received.
In the paragraphs you have just read I hope I have managed to show that filming specialised subjects need not be quite as boring as it may at first appear. There's

plenty of scope for variety. I have recalled a few of the many situations I have found myself involved in making specialist films on a host of different subjects. They seemed to work and, as a result, business continued increase. That situation has continued to this day and for that I shall always be immensely grateful.

6 - TIME OFF

As the productions I have described were completed our fledgling business continued to grow. We did not take on thousands of staff or make a bid for the BBC's television centre. The signs of our modest achievements were harder to detect. The bank manager smiled during our meetings and seemed to begin to have confidence in a venture which was at last bringing in the cash. When I first started trading, one of my competitors told me that in his view there are only two enjoyable moments in making films - signing a contract and sending out the bill. In his view, anything which happened between those two events as purely coincidental. I think he had a point!

We gradually managed to break into a world where doors are notoriously hard to open. I was fortunate in being able to attract some very loyal clients. I also had the support of a small team of extremely talented colleagues. For the first twenty years, most of my films were shot by Alistair Cameron – who was my business partner and who remains one of the finest cameramen in the world and a man who it has always been a pleasure to know and work with. For an equally long time my assistant–John Ballard, has kept me alive and succeeded in doing jobs which I thought were impossible to do. He is essentially practical and I am not. When something breaks down and I try to mend it, in due course a small army of expensive experts will have to be called in to put the damage right. When John is around, he has the knack of immediately being able to establish the cause of a problem. In an embarrassingly short time he usually manages to put it right. Together, with the help of a number of other colleagues who have joined us over the years, we have somehow managed to meet the demands of our audiences and clients around the world.

In the early years as business increased, we found we needed more space. After initially renting rooms, first by the hour and then on a longer-term basis, we managed to scrape enough cash together to acquire a three-year lease on the top floors of a building in London's Covent Garden. The area then housed Britain's premier fruit and vegetable market. It started trading in the early hours of the morning when people from all over the country came to buy vegetables, fruit and flowers. By 9am, when we arrived for work, most of their business had been completed.

Then Covent Garden was like a village. People still lived in flats above many of the fruit and vegetable shops. There was a unique atmosphere which has now entirely disappeared as outsiders have moved in and taken over. Today it's just another tourist attraction. We stayed in that building for many years, gradually taking over the leases for each floor until we had acquired the whole building. We built a 30-seat luxury cinema in the basement to preview our films, and put cutting rooms on each floor to cope with an ever increasing amount of work. They were great times and every Christmas we held a party to celebrate.

There was one party which I think anyone who attended it is unlikely to forget. For once we decided to try to be posh and impress our friends and clients. We had just taken possession of the whole building. It looked quite smart so we decided to invite guests to join us on a Saturday evening. To give the event a measure of prestige, we arranged to hire a uniformed official to check our guests' invitations and look suitably impressive at the entrance to our building. He arrived on time and looked incredibly smart. In his spotless uniform, with trousers pressed and a neatly trimmed moustache, no one could have failed to be impressed. When most of our guests had arrived, I felt rather guilty about this man, who was still standing there, looking rather bored as our friends continued to eat and drink. To cheer him up I decided to offer him a drink. He explained that he never normally drank on duty but would be "much obliged on this occasion." A glass of whisky was then produced and quietly placed near enough for him to reach when our guests were not looking. What I did not know at that time was that my colleagues, who had also felt sorry for this poor man, had made the same offer. On each occasion they had received the same reply. "Not normally.... but perhaps on this occasion." As the party reached its climax our prestige evaporated as he finally collapsed and fell down some stairs. When rescuers rushed to help him he was too drunk to stand up but miraculously revived when another glass was offered. I caught his last words as he was carried away. - "I would not normally but if you insist, perhaps just on this occasion!"

After that party I decided I needed a holiday. It wasn't just the party, as was rumoured at the time! Several years of very hard work had worn me out and I needed a break. Taking time off was something I had forgotten how to do, so when it came to making plans I did not know where to start. I browsed through the Sunday newspapers and eventually decided to try a type of holiday I had heard a lot about but had never experienced first hand. I aimed to investigate two British triumphs by flying to New York on Concorde and travelling back on the pride of the British fleet - the QE2.

As I am sure you know, only a few Concorde aircraft were ever built. Like so many great British ideas, it failed to live up to expectations. Ahead of its time in many ways, it lost its commercial impact because it made too much noise and carried relatively few passengers. That was sad, but for me the arrival of the world's first commercial supersonic aircraft was still an event worth celebrating and the best way of doing that was surely to book a flight on it.

I decided to book my flight with Air France as they flew Concordes and offered a deal which included a night in one of the best hotels in Paris. The five-star hotel was

furnished and run with a style one can only find in France. Many of the guests were French, which seemed to be a good omen as they presumably knew a lot more about Paris hotels than I did. There were also a fair number of people from other countries. They included a group of middle-aged American women whose conversations made it difficult to hear anything else when they were in the same room. They were a friendly bunch, and they were clearly out to enjoy themselves. Their zest for life was infectious and I wondered what had brought them to Paris. With some trepidation I approached the leader of the pack – a woman of doubtful age with purple hair and an orange shirt.
" You seem to be having fun. Are you in Paris for long?" I enquired.
"Gee, no," she replied. "We've finished now. We're just goin' home."
I asked where they and been.
"We've done Europe," she replied, smearing relish over a large hamburger which she was starting to devour. I wondered how long it had taken them to explore so many countries.
" Five days," I was informed.
" Have you been to England?" I enquired.
" Of course," she replied. "That was Thursday."
The rest of the group then joined in, recalling their Experiences of the few hours they had spent in England. They felt they knew everything that anyone could ever need to know. When they paused long enough for me to say another word, I thought I would ask what they felt they would remember most about their visit to Europe.
" You have visited seven different countries and seen some of the oldest signs of civilisation, and much more besides," I prompted. " If you had to select one thing you will always recall what would it be?"
For the first time there was silence. They all seemed to be lost in their own thoughts. At last the silence was

broken by the lady in the orange shirt.

"Gee, that's tough," she said, pausing a second. "But if you really press me I guess it would be the tiles in the washroom of our hotel, back in Venice!"

The following morning a car arrived to take me to board the eleven o'clock Concorde flight from Paris to New York. For me it was a wonderful experience throughout, though the vibration on take-off made me wonder if we would get into the air at all. Perhaps the De Gaulle Airport runway was at that time rougher than most, or maybe Concorde was an exceptionally light aircraft. I do not know where the explanation lies, but there seemed to be a lot of bumps and jolts as we raced along the tarmac. Once we were in the air, the flight was as any flight can be. As you will know if you were fortunate enough to have made made a similar journey, Concorde was quite a small aircraft. There were not many seats and I had feared it might be rather claustrophobic, but those fears soon proved to be without foundation. A glass of fine champagne as we departed, and superb service throughout the flight, ensured that every moment was a memorable occasion. The passenger who sat beside me had a much rougher time. He had also spent the previous night in Paris, where he had decided to emulate the French way of life by eating three plates of raw steak. He had been sick all night and boarded the plane looking like a ghost. As the best food and wines were served, and Concorde soared to great heights, he quietly covered his head with a blanket. There was little I could do, but I did manage to help him by eating the wonderful meal which he could not even bear to look at.

Several years later I picked up a newspaper and came face to face with front page pictures of a Concorde on fire as it took off from Paris. The paper contained Horrifying accounts of the aircraft's last minutes as it crashed ending the lives of everyone on board. I believe the French only bought five Concordes and have often wondered if the one that crashed was the aircraft that I flew on that day.

I arrived at New York at eight o'clock in the morning – three hours earlier than I had left Paris! A car was waiting to drive to a hotel where I stayed for a few days before boarding the QE2 for to sail back to Britain.

The Queen Elizabeth 2, which in those days was one of the largest ships afloat, was even then in many ways almost a memorial to a bygone age. The service and facilities were reasonably up-to-date, but there remained an air of life in the sixties, when the great ship was built and set sail on a disastrous maiden voyage. The engines broke down and the pride of Britain's fleet returned to port for new turbine blades and other changes, which took many months to complete. In her later years QE2 became a cult and attracted people from all over the world and many walks of life.

On any cruise or transatlantic crossing, what the brochures promise and what you actually encounter may not be the same. A lot depends on where you are heading and who you are traveling with. Your destination, any intermediate ports of call and your fellow passengers will to some extent affect your enjoyment on route.

On QE2, there was then a marked difference between a transatlantic crossing and a cruise round Europe, the Caribbean or any other ports. The ship was always officially a one-class vessel. That is true was true in as much as any passenger had the run of the ship throughout the voyage, but there was another point which potential travelers may needed to bear in mind. Passengers could eat in four different restaurants. Two were extremely smart. They were known as "The Grills." There was also a slightly less grand restaurant and another one for passengers who paid the cheapest fares. Both were named after former Cunard ships –The Caronia (intermediate grade) and The Mauretania. Transatlantic crossings seemed to attract a greater mix of people and, in my

experience, a higher standard of food and service.
In The Grills, on the transatlantic run I was told that you could ask the chefs to prepare almost anything you care to mention. With a day's notice, they would usually be happy to comply. I always found the food and service aboard was better than in most five star hotels ashore, but that does not mean that the efforts of those who provide such excellent service are always appreciated. On my first transatlantic crossing I found myself sitting at a large table with several other passengers. They were good company throughout the voyage but they were undoubtedly a pretty weird mix. Unlike me, they were all extremely rich. They had also been on the ship a great many times. On one side there was a large American who happened to own a bank. He was accompanied by a very jolly wife. They had been married for years, Obviously loved each other, and enjoyed life. Next to them there were two Scottish sisters of advancing age. They said very little and ate even less. As the voyage progressed, I discovered that the more lively of the two had been married to a man who had died a few months before. She had managed to persuade her sister to Accompany her on the trip. She had never married and had spent most of her life managing the affairs of her local church, in a part of Scotland where the only other inhabitants appear to have been highland sheep. She was a strange companion. She rarely spoke and would only eat boiled chicken. In one of the finest restaurants in the world, that seemed a pity but she said she had enjoyed the same food for years and did not intend to change. As she only uttered a few words in the course of the voyage, she was not the easiest person to get to know. Fortunately her sister, and the others at the table, made up for that.
As we approached Southampton at the end of our journey, our silent companion leaned across the table and whispered in my ear her one revelation on the whole

trip:
" I hate ships and I don't like America!" Her fare had cost her over seven thousand pounds - A pretty substantial sum in those days As the last portion of boiled chicken landed on her plate, I found myself wondering if she thought the money had been well spent.

I met entirely different people when I later joined QE2 for two short cruises – one in Europe and another in the Caribbean. The first of those trips introduced me to one of the most unforgettable characters I have ever met. The second made newspaper headlines - for reasons totally unconnected with me - so I will briefly recall what I encountered.

The Euro cruise started in Southampton. It was a cut price affair by QE standards. The menus even included shepherd's pie – a basic UK dish which is a long way away from the champagne and caviar style of fare which some transatlantic passengers seem to be unable to exist without. We were on board for two weeks called at a number of ports. Gibraltar, to meet the apes and buy drinks at encouragingly low prices. Tenerife at Easter, to find that everything was shut. And finally Lanzarotte, to discover just how boring a volcanic island which is invaded by ancient tourists can manage to be.

It was a pretty basic cruise but it was fun because there were some great people aboard. On a ship as big as QE2, one of the plus points of cruising is that you do not have to get involved in anything if you do not wish to do so. There was an excellent library and plenty of deck space so it was perfectly easy, and acceptable, to sit quietly on your own, whenever you wished. Today there are many cruise lines which still have to learn the value of that.

On our third day at sea I began to notice a passenger who always seemed to be standing on deck at exactly the same point, looking out to sea. He was tall and smartly dressed and he hardly moved at all. I could only see his back view. When I arrived on deck each morning, he was already there. When others went below for meals, he stayed where he was. As the voyage progressed, I found myself wondering who this man was, and what he was doing there. In a ship with so many amenities, it seemed odd that anyone should choose to remain virtually motionless, in the same place on an open deck, day after day staring out to sea. Eventually I decided to approach him and pass the time of day. That decision changed the whole voyage for me, and it significantly affected my attitude to life.

I moved across the deck and found myself standing next to a man who was about fifty years old. He had a suntanned face and he was wearing sunglasses.

" Lovely day isn't it?" I mumbled.

"It certainly is. The best we've had so far," he replied in a voice which went well with the image created by his smart jacket, collar and tie. We chatted for a while. He told me he was enjoying the voyage and was travelling alone. It was the first time he had been on a cruise and he felt it was something everyone should try. He had found there was so much to enjoy. We went on to chat about how we had booked the trip and the prices we had paid. And then he explained that he had had great difficulty booking anything at all. It had taken him a year to get aboard. A year of battles he would prefer to forget. I was about to enquire why, when he removed his sunglasses and I saw that he was blind.

At that particular moment we were passing one of the most picturesque points on the voyage. Gibraltar was emerging from the mists of a Mediterranean dawn. It took me a while to gather my thoughts. There was I, able to enjoy all the pleasures of life, and this man alongside me could see absolutely nothing. Over the next few days I was to learn that my assessment of the situation was entirely wrong. He was so much better than I could ever be. He could not see, but every sound made its own impression. He was an achiever and had made a success of life with little help from anyone. As we got to know each other, I started to try to describe some of the views and the scenes we passed. He gradually, and at first Reluctantly began to reveal a few things about himself. He had been born blind and had learned Braille well enough to win a university place. He was clearly bright, for he had gone on to take up a career in the professions. He had a job, which many sighted people would not have the qualifications to do. I will not reveal the nature of his profession for he has since become a well known public figure and I have no wish to embarrass him in any way. For me he will remain one of life's really great achievers. When he said he wanted to take a cruise, the shipping companies he had approached opposed every move. They were worried about the safety implications of allowing a sightless person to board their ships where steps and other obstructions were to be found everywhere. He persisted and won. He taught me so much. I have not met him since that memorable voyage, but he is in my mind's eye every day. A wonderful man who put life in perspective and, against all the odds, managed to achieve far more than most.

Some years after that encounter, I found myself aboard QE2 again. I flew to New York to join what the UK press was then describing as "the cruise from hell". QE2 had sailed from Southampton after a refit and run straight into a force ten gale which followed her across the Atlantic. It was very rough indeed. As those who travelled on that occasion will recall, Cunard who then owned the ship, had not managed to complete the refit on time. QE2 put to sea with a significant amount of work still to be done. The situation was considered so grave that several hundred passengers, who had booked cabins which remained in an un-inhabitable condition, were left at Southampton and not allowed to board. Unhelpful statements from a company spokesman made matters worse and by the time the ship arrived in New York, what

should have been a relatively small problem had become front page news in the international press.
In New York we waited for the ship to arrive. Because of the rough seas it was almost a day late. When it eventually docked we were not sure if we would be allowed aboard. We had booked (and paid for) quite good cabins on what was supposed to be a Christmas treat, but with all the scares in the press we did not know what to expect. We eventually boarded a day late, to be received with the courteous service I have always found on Cunard ships. Ashore the world's press waited and everyone was complaining. On board it was clear that some things were wrong. The swimming pool was piled high with rubbish. So many cabins had been flooded due to plumbing leaks, that the crew had started using a code word - "Niagara" - to alert each other to the latest crisis. The US authorities impounded the ship until essential safety work had been completed. We eventually sailed a couple of days late, but that was the only real problem we encountered. I, my companion, and most of the other passengers aboard were able to make allowances for the few problems that still remained. When things went wrong, the exhausted crew did everything possible to put matters right. We woke one morning to find the floor of our cabin was under water. At first we wondered if we had hit another iceberg but we soon realised that the flood was just another result of the incomplete refit. Cunard looked after us very well. Of course not everyone was happy. One lady created hell and threatened to sue when she flushed a toilet which overflowed and allegedly ruined her dress!
It was on that voyage that I met a man who shared the same profession as the blind man I had met on my earlier trip. They had similar jobs, but they had nothing else in common. The Christmas cruise character was one of those people who firmly believes that he was always right about everything. He was extremely wealthy and eager to

make more by exploiting every possible opportunity. He was happy to ignore the many good things the ship's crew did for him and his family, and caused trouble by complaining about everything to anyone who would listen when we arrived at each port. He was a pain to have on board and I hope subsequent experiences in life have taught him the vital lessons he obviously needed to learn. My first holiday cruise was arranged for fun and relaxation but it also made me think that perhaps we could extend our business by making films for cruise lines and holiday companies. We moved into that sector a few months later and have remained there, on a fairly selective basis, ever since. Perhaps you think that holiday films must be great fun to make. If that is your view, perhaps I can change it with a few simple facts.

Going on holiday is one thing. Filming other people on holiday is quite another. The first major difference is that, as you are being paid to make the film, the organisation which is footing the bill wants its views put across. Those views can sometimes be difficult to accommodate. The images holiday companies attempt to create are not always the same as the realities you encounter. I was once invited to make a film for long-established English south coast resort. The town was smart and quite elite. It was also well known for the age of the people who returned there year after year. When a new director of tourism was appointed, he wanted to change that image overnight and project a picture of a town seething with life and full of modern tourist attractions. As there were only a handful of leisure amenities, and the average age of the customers in the town was around sixty-five, it was soon clear that meeting his requirements was likely to be an uphill task! On the comparatively rare occasions when one does find a holiday company which takes an realistic approach to marketing, making a good film in the time available can still be very hard work. When the job has been completed and you return to base, everyone thinks

you have been living it up or lying on a beach. In reality you may well have been filming twenty hours a day, Trying to cover all the points the sponsor wants audiences to see. Finding the right locations is the first problem. You have to be there at the right time on the right day. After a while you begin to hear the same words again and again
. "You should have been here yesterday." No matter how well your schedule is planned, something better always seems to have happened the day before you arrived. The sun was shining. The beach looked less crowded. There were nicer-looking people or there was some activity which cannot now be repeated. It can all be very frustrating, especially when you are working for a company which expects the earth and has very little idea of what is actually involved in making a film. You can spend hours trying to get a single shot. You have to wait for the light to be right or for the background to be clear of unwanted obstructions. That idyllic looking child over there would make a great shot if the refuse lorry in the background would just move away. The young couple enjoying those cocktails with the paper umbrellas would make a great picture, if one could just avoid showing the drunk slumped across the bar. You have to wait, sometimes for hours, to get a few seconds of useable film. Making cruise films you can run into a number of problems. Some ships, especially older ones, can look very tatty if your pictures are not carefully framed. You will often find people who have had too much to drink. They think they are wonderful and go to great lengths to be filmed, but you have to be tactful and leave them out. Some people go on holiday with girlfriends, wives or people who are not their usual partners, and one has to try not to shoot any scenes which might be misunderstood or could be used as evidence in a court. It's a tough job but, if it is produced properly, a promotional video can prove to be a goldmine for a sponsor's point of view.

One of our first holiday ventures was a commission to make a film about cruising on the Rhine. It sounds wonderful, doesn't it! It turned out to be four weeks of sheer hell. In those days there were a limited number of companies operating cruises, which started in Amsterdam, travelled to Basel and then went back again. Our commission came from a smallish company at the top end of the market. They were a first-class outfit but we joined them at the wrong time. It rained almost every day and thick mists obscured the views we were trying to film. We moved from one boat to another, up and down the length of the Rhine and prayed for good weather, but our prayers were ignored. The river rose to exceptionally high levels and several of the towns we were due to visit were under water by the time we arrived. The Conditions made out-door filming impossible so we shot as much as we could in the bar, lounge and restaurant. The standard of food and service aboard was high and most of the passengers seemed to be enjoying themselves. Carl - the manager in charge of catering, had been in the business for years. He had seen it all before and knew how to cope whatever happened, which proved to be just as well on the night we decided to film a formal dinner in the main restaurant.

We were approaching Cologne as dinner was served. Waiters carrying two hundred steaks on silver trays arrived just as the fast-running tide threw the boat violently off course. We hit the riverbank with considerable force. Waiters flew in all directions and their silver platters crashed to the floor. The passengers, who remained seated, escaped uninjured but the carpet was quickly littered with food.

When situations like that occur, you soon find out if a company is good at dealing with emergencies. On this occasion the passengers could not fail to be impressed. As the boat steadied, Carl moved to a microphone and apologised for what he described as "that small interruption." Before anyone could complain he hastened to reassure them.

"Of course on this ship we are prepared for any emergency. We carry ample supplies for all so please bear with us, and in ten minutes a freshly cooked meal will be served."

The customers were delighted. A round of applause echoed round the room as we filmed lots of happy people sitting at their tables. When things had calmed down I decided to pop into the kitchen to see how they were coping. Carl was there, as always, quietly but indisputably in command.

"That was all very impressive," I told him. "The passengers are over the moon. You must be well organised to replace two hundred steaks at the drop of a hat." He smiled and pointed to a corner of the kitchen where staff were frantically washing steaks under a tap and heating them under a grill and coating them with parsley. Ten minutes later the waiters returned in triumph. That was one a meal we did not show in our finished film!

We completed our river cruise assignment two weeks later than we had originally planned because of the weather. It had been a difficult job but the end result was well received and produced customers for the cruise line until it was taken over by a much larger company. Our next holiday film took us further to the Indian Ocean and the lovely island of Sri Lanka.

Sri Lanka, which was known as Ceylon for many years, is officially a third world country. It is not a major financial power but it is a wonderful place and one I can unhesitatingly recommend. In recent years a civil war has divided the island. They have also suffered from a devastating flood but the spirit of the people is undimmed and it is still a great place to visit. Sri Lanka is an island I would be happy to return to at any time.

I first went there to make a film. We had been chosen by

the Sir Lanka Government, who had looked at videos made by American, French, German and Japanese companies and eventually decided that they liked what we did enough to award us a contract. I arrived at Colombo airport with a small film crew not knowing what we were likely to find. The drive into Colombo put things in context. Bullock carts and ancient Morris minors jostled for position on pot-holed roads. The scene appeared to have changed very little for at least thirty years. Our client came to our hotel the following morning.

Like virtually all the Sri Lankans we met in the course of several visits, the Director of Tourism was full of charm and a pleasure to be with. We had quoted quite a low price for making our film but it soon became clear that by Sri Lankan standards even that figure was regarded as a considerable sum. "Do you realize", our client asked when we first met," that for the money we are paying you we could almost build a hospital?" As the sum would barely cover the production of a thirty-second TV commercial in Europe I was suitably shocked and resolved to work as hard as I could from that moment on. For three weeks we toured the country, travelling by taxi and in a hired car. The taxi was the most fun. If it travelled at more than twenty miles an hour it filled with blue smoke and bits started to fall off. Hardboard panels, which had replaced the original doors many years ago, rattled encouragingly as we bumped along. I don't think there were any brakes but we never moved fast enough to find out. When we wanted to stop, we just glided to a halt, got out and started to film.

We watched fishermen, standing on stilts, catching more fish than many would with all the latest gear. We filmed as the fish they caught were auctioned on the beach in scenes which would not have been out of place in an Ealing comedy. At one point we were provided with a Sri Lankan air force helicopter to speed us on our way. When fuel ran low, we landed on what looked like a completely derelict piece of land. Our pilot - a very young Sri Lankan air force captain, explained that it had been an aerodrome during the war but was now only used for emergency refuelling. As we landed people on old bicycles emerged from all directions. Rusty fuel drums were wheeled out from under some bushes. With the aid of a hand pump and a few basic tools, the helicopter was then refuelled. We took off again and found we were heading for a storm. At that time of year, thunderstorms are a pretty rare occurrence. As jet-black clouds engulfed us I thought our pilot was looking rather concerned. The plane was being quite violently thrown around and rain and lightning filled the air. I was sitting in the co-pilot's seat, as we were flying with a one-man crew. As the storm gathered strength, the pilot leaned across and quietly mentioned that he was not sure if the altimeter was working as we were using what had been a standby plane. After that news he was not the only one who was sweating! Fortunately the clouds soon parted and we are able to make an unscheduled landing on a cricket pitch in the middle of a match.

For years Sri Lanka used to supply much of the world with tea, and even today its tea industry still plays an important part in the local economy. I had never visited a tea plantation and was eager to include one in our film. Sri Lanka is a tropical island and when we arrived to film the daytime temperature was very hot indeed. Tea grows best in a cool climate, so the island's tea Plantations are to be found in what the local people call their mountains. They are not particularly high but, as you drive from sea level up into the hills, the climate completely changes. Green becomes the predominant colour and the heat of the sun dies away. After climbing narrow hillside roads for twenty minutes, we got our first view of a major tea plantation. As you probably know, tea grows on bushes and from our viewpoint bushes stretched as far as the eye could see. It is still picked by hand. Teams of girls in colourful clothes select the best leaves and throw them over their shoulders into baskets which they carry on their backs. It's delightfully old Fashioned and very picturesque.

We had arranged to meet the manager of the estate at the main factory building, where baskets of tea are brought to be weighed. Our host turned out to be a short man with a permanent ear-to-ear grin. He had worked on this plantation all his life and was now responsible for all its activities. He was naturally proud of everything we saw and he took us on an extended tour of each department. We saw baskets being weighed and learned that tea grown near the top of a hill tends to be stronger than that picked on the lower slopes. We watched as experts tasted samples made from a host of different leaves. Time after time we were reminded that quality and cleanliness were the keys to making the perfect tea. It was an interesting and rather exhausting morning. As our tour ended, the manager invited us to join him and his wife at their home –The Bungalow– for "some traditional hospitality." By then we were all dying for a gin and we set off for the bungalow with high hopes.

Our host's home would have put even the most garish Indian restaurant to shame. I have never seen such a proliferation of bright orange and red flocked wallpaper. The furniture was modern plastic and painted ducks hung from the walls. Our host welcomed us inside and told us he was sure we must be ready for a drink. We were not going to argue, but the refreshment we had hoped for failed to arrive.

"You have seen everything we do, but you have not yet had a chance to enjoy our finished products," the manager said, as his wife entered the room carrying a tray on which there was a cat-shaped teapot and four plastic mugs. "Now we can put that right and then you will appreciate just how fine our teas really are". We watched as the mugs were filled with tea. Before we could pick them up, the manager produced a tin of sweetened condensed milk and poured a generous portion into each mug. The delicate flavour we had been hearing about for the entire morning was totally destroyed and the resulting drink was one of the most revolting I have ever encountered. Feeling quite sick after walking for hours and drinking sweet tea, I asked if I might use the lavatory. I was shown to a room slightly larger than a fridge. By turning sideways I was just able to get inside. Facing the lavatory, I lifted the seat but before I could perform, a huge frog leaped out of the bowl and climbed up my shirt. I turned and fled. For some reason I find the rest of our visit is less easy to recall!

On our last day in Sri Lanka we had arranged to take a few shots of aircraft landing at Colombo airport. We walked across the grass, which covered the area between the runway and the main terminal building. As a jumbo jet hit the tarmac our camera rolled and we got a nice shot as it sped towards us, with the sun setting in a spectacular blaze of colours in the background. We were pleased with what was scheduled to be the last shot on that assignment. Carrying our equipment we walked back through the grass towards the terminal building. Our contact man was in the bar waiting for us. When we told him where we had been, he exploded with a mixture of emotion and rage.

" Do you know what you just done?" he asked, as we tried to work out what could possibly be amiss.

"We have just finished the last shot", I replied as innocently as I could.

" It could have been the last shot you will ever film," he replied. I assumed we had broken some airport rule or stood too near the runway, and was ready to apologise but I did not get the chance." Come with me", he commanded.

We meekly followed him, expecting to be arrested at any

moment. We walked through the terminal building and headed for a small shack, which stood nearby. As we reached the door our guide produced a large bunch of keys, I thought we were going to be locked up and asked where we were.

The shack door was opened and we were told to step inside. We found ourselves in a small room which was very dimly lit. On every wall there were glass display cases and in each case there was a dead snake.

"See those?" our guide asked, still shaking with emotion. "Every one of them is poisonous and the smallest is only three inches long. It can kill anyone in seconds."

It was all very interesting but I could not see why it concerned us. I soon found out, as he went on to explain that the snakes we were looking at had all been found in the grassy area we had walked through a few minutes ago!

Today that film has become a collector's item. Though the north of the island has changed considerably as a result of recent Tamil Tigers conflicts, Sri Lanka as a whole remains a delightfully unspoiled place and the welcome visitors receive remains genuine and cordial. The film ,though it is dated by modern standards, continues to capture the spirit of the place so well that it has recently been restored and re-released on DVD.

There we no snakes to be found in the next place we visited and it was much nearer home. I had heard of the Channel Islands but had never had a chance to visit them. One day I got a telephone call from the director of tourism on Guernsey - the second largest Channel Island. It is around twenty miles long and it lies a few miles off the coast of France. He had seen some of our films and wanted to know if his committee could come and meet us when they visited London later that week.

In due course they arrived and explained that they needed an up-to-date tourist film. Would we be interested in making it? I had done some research before they arrived and had already learned enough to realise that Guernsey seemed to be a very pleasant place. There was no guarantee that we would get the job. As always we had to come up with ideas we could we could produce within our client's budget. We nearly lost the chance even to compete when we met the full tourist committee for the first time.

A friend, who had lived on the island, had warned me to be prepared." They're a tough bunch," he had advised. "They're islanders born and bred and they're all teetotal. Whatever you do, don't offer them a drink." I took the advice seriously.

When the committee arrived, its members seemed to me to be exceptionally nice. We got on well, but I heeded the advice on alcohol and, when our meeting ended only offered them soft drinks.

A month later when we were awarded the contract we had sought, I discovered that the friend who had advised me had been having a joke. The committee members were not teetotal. When we got to know them better they told us that and our failure to offer suitable hospitality during their visit to London had been the only negative outcome of our first encounter. They had returned to Guernsey assuming that we did not drink, and the prospect of working with any company on that basis had nearly cost us the job. Fortunately the true facts emerged in time and we began an association with Guernsey that was to continue for many years.

We have filmed in Guernsey on numerous occasions. In summer we have often been lucky and enjoyed hours of sunshine. There have also been days when mists have come down. The island's airport has remained closed and ships have sounded their sirens as they put to sea. Residents can enjoy many benefits. Income tax was then low and there were no death duties or an inheritance tax. Visitors could also benefit from the absence of VAT. Our job was to show Guernsey's tourist attractions in an interesting way, and to try to capture the spirit of the place. You don't have to spend long on Guernsey to see why the island is unique. The pressures of mainland life are swept away the moment you land. Fresh air, good food and people who have time to smile and chat are everywhere.

My first real encounter with the local people set the tone for all the other dealings I have had with them over the years. We had arrived to film one of the main events of the year – the battle of flowers. It takes place every summer. Floral displays of all shapes and sizes are built up on floats on the night before the main event is due to proceed. It is all done with a reasonable degree of secrecy so designs cannot be copied. We wanted to film the building of the floats but we did not know where to find them. We hired a car and started to drive slowly round the island.

The roads on Guernsey are quite narrow and we were moving slowly, so we could peer over hedges and see what was going on. In a few minutes a long queue of cars built up behind us as the road was too narrow for anyone to pass. We eventually reached a point which was slightly wider. One of the cars, which had now been trapped behind us for at least five minutes, shot past and halted abruptly a few yards ahead. As I watched the driver, who was a tall well built man, got out and walked towards me. When he reached our car he turned to face me. I can still recall his exact words.

"You look as if you're lost. Can I help you?"

That reaction was typical of Guernsey and the wonderful people who live there. On our first visit we spent three weeks filming some of the island's many attractions. We visited the smallest church in the world and scores of unspoiled bays, beaches and cliff walks. We also filmed an international power boat race where the main attraction for me was from a different age.

The harbour at St Peter Port was full of world class

power boats and hundreds of expensive yachts but for me the main attraction lay elsewhere. In a corner of the bay, a middle-aged man was trying to light the boiler of a small steam driven craft. It was old and slightly faded until the boiler got up steam. Then it chugged into life. The name on the stern was one which any film fan should instantly recall. The boat was called *"The African Queen."*
We decided to investigate and, when it approached the shore, we were able to meet its present owner. He was an businessman who owned a large Florida hotel. In the course of a busy life, he had achieved considerable success in a number of ventures but his main interest now was *The African Queen*. He had found her in a derelict state in an African swamp. He recalled how fine she had looked when Humphrey Bogart and Katharine Hepburn had been aboard, making the film, which eventually took its name from this small craft. He felt there was only one thing he could do. He had to restore her. It took him months and cost a fortune. At last his goal was achieved and he was able to spend much of his time travelling round the world, so others could enjoy the results of his efforts. To bring the boat to Guernsey he had chartered a jumbo jet. We included *The African Queen* in our film and had the pleasure of spending time with its new owner, a man who seemed to me to have an interesting approach to life.
The Guernsey Government is also responsible for three other islands – Alderney, Herm and Sark. They were also included in our film. They are all enchanting in their Different ways. Alderney is famous for its sea birds and for a proliferation of bars, which led one unkind commentator to describe the islanders as "a bunch of alcoholics clinging to a rock." It is an inaccurate description of very pleasant people and a delightful spot. Herm – the smallest of the islands – at that time was run under licence by a family team. It's a sort of Robinson Crusoe place which deliberately ignores the passing of

time. Sark is well known because no one on the island is allowed to use a car. When a doctor applied to live on Sark, he asked for a special dispensation in view of the nature of his work. On that one occasion, permission was granted. He was told that he could bring his car, with one proviso. It must always be drawn by a horse!

As aircraft are forbidden to fly across Sark, let alone land there, visitors must arrive by sea. They are met at the foot of a cliff by tractors and trailers which then transport everyone to the top of a hill. They can then continue their journeys on one of the Islanders' many horse drawn carts.

On a fine day Sark is a great place to be. Life there had changed remarkably little over the years. The Islanders make their own laws and have their own parliament, which meets from time to time under the Chairmanship of the island's number one citizen - Le Seigneur. His name is Michael Beaumont. When his predecessor, The Dame of Sark, died Beaumont and his wife were living in England, where he earned his living helping to design commercial aircraft. The news that he had inherited the title of Seigneur of Sark must have come as quite a shock. They moved to the island and settled in. Now they are greatly respected by those who live in, and visit, this unique place. Their new life is not entirely without its compensations. The Seigneur is the only person who is allowed to keep pigeons on the island! The feudal situation has recently been challenged but Sark remains a delightful place to visit.

I have always enjoyed my visits to Guernsey and have returned over the years to make a number of films. One of the hardest to produce turned out to be one of the most successful, as often proves to be the case. When I was asked to make a film telling the history of the Bailiwick my first thoughts were that that it would be an impossible task. Bringing history to life on film without an enormous budget is never easy. It is tempting to rely on ancient documents and people talking to camera and end up with an extremely in a boring end product. *ECHOES OF THE PAST* took us six weeks to make .It told the story of the islands from the very early days when smugglers worked in what is now St Peter Port. It also explored the main events of the second world war when the s islands were the only British territories occupied by the |Germans.

The finished film included s eye witness accounts of what life the was like then. As many of the people who provided those accounts have now died the film has become a collector's item. It has recently been digitally restored and is now available on DVD.

As time passed, our fledgling business continued to grow. Much to my surprise, we found we were getting a lot of repeat business. Some people never learn! Our loyal customers seemed to come back to us again and again, and that was good because it meant that we did not have to advertise. Of course not everything went exactly as we planned. We had a few disasters but I did not feel they were our fault then and, in retrospect, I believe that assessment was probably correct. It takes two to tango and at least two to agree the treatment and script for any worthwhile film.

On a very few occasions we met people who knew what they wanted but would not listen to anyone else, and that can be a recipe for disaster. To make a successful film you need good teamwork. The director, writers and technicians must work well together to ensure a good end result. If the film you are making is designed to promote a particular product or service, the sponsor, who is paying the bill, must have confidence in that team. If that confidence isn't there, you can have problems from the start, as I was to discover when we made one of our biggest disasters.

The marketing director of a company making flat pack boxed kitchens, which people could assemble themselves, approached us after seeing some of our films. He told me he wanted to make "a half hour film to promote the sale of our products". His aim was simple enough. He wanted to show the range of kitchens his company could supply and convince people that they could be assembled with ease by anyone at home A brochure and some leaflets had already been prepared but sales had failed to take off. We soon discovered why.

Our self styled marketing expert was one of those unhappy people who knows all about everything. The kitchen units he wanted to sell were built to his designs. The brochure and leaflets were written by him. They showed pictures of him at least three times on every page. In the film he had commissioned, he wanted to use the same approach. He insisted on writing a script and checking every shot through the camera viewfinder before it was filmed.

" I know what I am doing," he kept telling us. The sad thing was that he really believed it, and that could only lead one way. You will not be surprised to know that Mr Knowall wanted to present the film himself. He insisted that in most of our shots he should be seen speaking directly to camera. He had a dull voice and looked and sounded half-dead but he was convinced that he would soon be on his way to pock up an Oscar. Suggestions on how scenes could be filmed to show the kitchens at their best were swept aside. A film was eventually put together and Mr Knowall went merrily on his way and those involved in the production asked to have their names left off the credits.

I heard nothing more for quite a while then our client called us to complain. Audiences were apparently failing to respond to his new marketing investment and he could not understand why. Fortunately there are very few people like poor Mr Knowall!

When you make promotional films you expect your clients to know what they want but most clients welcome advice on the best way to put their ideas across, using a medium they accept they do not know much about. They realise that making films on even the most basic subjects requires a variety of skills. If a script is written like a sales brochure, it will never sound right. Getting that message across can sometime be a battle. Over the years it's a battle I have fought a good many times. Sometimes I have won and sometimes I have lost and is is the memory of one of those occasions that upsets me most.

We had been approached by a company which was well known for making protective safety boots. They wanted a video which they could use as a sales promotional aid. I was invited to visit their factories and meet the company's key personnel. They made high quality products and they were very pleasant people but the only promotional activity they had ever undertaken was producing a basic sales brochure. It contained pictures of boots in various styles accompanied by a list of prices. They wanted us to make a film in the same basic way. It was to be a catalogue of the company's products with a straightforward commentary making the sales points the company wanted to get across. I was not keen to make anything like that and asked s if they would consider doing something a little more ambitious. They agreed to give it a try and I was commissioned to come up with some fresh ideas.

I spent a long time trying to find ideas which I felt would work. It's an exercise you might perhaps care to try yourself. Imagine you have been asked to make a film about protective safety boots. How would you go about it ? You will soon find that it is not an easy subject to bring to life. In those days many industrially sponsored films had commentaries read by the sort of voices one normally associates with the newsreels of the past. They were calm, impartial and authoritative. Pictures showed the products while a narrator covered all the necessary sales points. The end result was often deadly dull but it was what many sponsors wanted and insisted they got. I wanted to break away from that dreadful format and decided to write the commentary for the film I envisaged so in stead of being spoken by a formal narrator it could appear to be being spoken by the voice of a man's feet. They were very upset because their owner made life hell and took them for granted. Every day at work he but put their safety at risk time after time. To make the treatment work I decided to try to shoot every shot at floor level, so audiences would see what the voice was describing as if the feet had eyes as well as a voice. It was fun developing the feet into a real character and, with the right voice reading the lines. I was confident that it was an the idea which would work.

It took me several weeks to perfect a script. I tested my idea on a number of colleagues and they all loved it. More time was then spent perfecting the words and I began to feel that at last the concept had potential. To me the success of the film would entirely depend on being able to get the right voice. We needed a first class actor who could bring our character to life. He must be able to get a laugh at times and also get a serious message across. I had one very special voice in mind.

At the time Kenneth Williams was at the peak of his career. He was working all hours of the day and night. He was on stage starring in a west end theatre every night. His mornings were spent at the BBC recording *JUST A MINUTE* and other immensely popular radio shows. When he was not doing that he was at Pinewood studios starring in *CARRY ON* films for which he was being paid £500 a day. With so many commitments and successes I did not expect him to be interested in becoming the voice of a character I had created to boost the sales of safety footwear! I nearly abandoned the idea without approaching him but eventually decided that at least I could do was ask. I sent him a script and a brief

covering note. He read the words and, much to my delight, said he would love to do it.
We decided to record the soundtrack before any pictures were shot. On the appointed day Kenny arrived at the Oxford street recording studio we always used to record our soundtracks. He arrived early and immaculately dressed in gray flannel trousers and a tweed sports jacket. We had never met before and I was then still in my twenties I was quite nervous about working with a man who had already has such a distinguished career. We spent an hour discussing the script and then made an excellent recording. Kenny was wonderfully professional to work with. He was quite a serious a person in real life without any great sense of humour but in front of a microphone he instantly came to life and could turn into whoever you wanted him to be. He knew exactly what techniques to use to make his voice sound right from every angle. He did a wonderful job and made the character we had created seem interesting and funny.
A few days later I took the recording down to play it to the sponsors of our film. The managing director listed and then nearly had a fit. He completely lost his cool and accused me of trying to send up the company he had built up over many years and make people laugh at his expense. For the first time I realised that he had no sense of humour. Our contract was cancelled the very next day. Weeks later the company made a completely straightforward film with a conventional commentary. It sold their products. They were happy but what could have been a masterpiece ended in a bin. Over the years I have tried to believe that customers are always right but on that occasion I must admit I had my doubts and I still have!
 Several years after the Kenneth Williams incident I was introduced to another character who had very definite views. Her name was Margaret Thatcher and at the time she was Britain's Prime Minister. Our first encounter was on the day which I think must have been the most

worrying that she experienced in her entire career. It was the first day of Falkland war.

Weeks earlier we had been commissioned to produce a film for a company which was based in the Prime Minister's Finchley constituency. One of her constituents - Michael Gerson- had started an overseas removals firm and run it successfully for 21 years. To celebrate that milestone the company was going to open a huge new warehouse. As Mr Gerson had been a keen supporter of the conservative party for many years, Mrs Thatcher had agreed to perform the opening ceremony and we had been asked to record the occasion.

When plans for that day had first been made most of us had never even heard of the Falklands. When the day finally arrived and we suddenly found we were facing a war, Britain and Mrs Thatcher were headline news around the world. That morning as we prepared to set out to met our contractual commitments, we expected to hear that the opening ceremony had been cancelled before we arrived. As no message was received we set out to travel to Mr Gerson's warehouse. We arrived to find the world's television networks clamouring at the gates. Every reporter from miles around had arrived hoping to capture what had always been destined to be a private occasion for Gerson's customers and staff.

We duly reported for duty and discovered that as far as anyone was aware everything that had been planned was still likely to go ahead. We were told that at 11 o'clock Mrs Thatcher would chair a cabinet meeting in Downing street. She had promised to travel to Finchley immediately after that, as she had originally arranged. Husband Dennis would arrive earlier.

With the country at war and the world's media creating havoc on the other side of barred gates we are beginning to appreciate how fortunate we were. We were going to be able to record a unique occasion which was not open to the press on what was possibly going to be the most crucial day in the Prime Minister's career. It seemed like a dream and frankly I still doubted that anything would ever happen.

Exactly on time Mr Thatcher arrived driving his own Ford car. He parked it and chatted to his hosts with the informality he always seemed to be able to mange and enjoy. He assured us that the Prime Minister would undoubtedly arrive and would make her way there as soon as the cabinet meeting had ended. We watched and waited and then she arrived. She was completely calm, made an excellent impromptu speech and stayed for well over an hour. A commemorative tablet was unveiled and then she took her place in the warehouse where tables had been laid for a formal lunch. As the proceedings ended we all stood up and sang *Land of Hope and Glory*. If I had not been working so hard to help my crew to capture the event for our client, I would probably have been in tears. It was a privilege to be present at such a unique moment in the country's history.

As the years passed our business continued to grow. Competitors began to feel the heat and some well established names, which had caused us great concern when we first started, suddenly found they could no longer compete. Our activities were beginning to arouse the interest of businesses we had tried work with before. Now they were approaching us. Among those we were to hear from was one of Britain's biggest household names . It was the AA – The Automobile Association. At that time largest organisation in the world specifically created to help motorists and other road users.

The AA was started in 1905 by a visionary lawyer called Stenson Cooke. Then motoring was still relatively new. Horse drawn busses and bicycles were the most common means of transport. Wealthy people who had the money to invest in what many regarded as a dangerous new invention were often regarded as a menace. Laws designed to curb their freedom had come into force as early as 1896. Then it decreed that any motors on a highway must be preceded by a man on foot carrying a red flag. A later act published in 1903 declared that speed itself was to be an offence regardless of danger.

To enforce the laws as they were passed police on bicycles ambushed motorists who they felt had driven too fast over a measured mile. Stenson Cooke felt the laws were too harsh and something should be done to protect the interests of motorists. He formed a committee which recruited a number of friends who owned bicycles. They noted where police patrols were working and flagged down approaching motorists to and warned them before they could be caught. They wore armbands which identified them as member of what was soon to became known as The Automobile Association

We first got involved with the AA in the 1960s when we are asked to asked a film about the services the organisation was offering at that time. Then it was in its prime. An enormous, well run organisation which helped motorists and other road users in many different ways. A breakdown service assisting drivers who had run into trouble on was the core business. Route maps were prepared so journeys could be planned and the basic services offered were expanded in many ways which in the years before mobile phones and satellite communication were often a lifeline to anyone who used the roads. By the time our film – *AA THE SIGN FOR SERVICE-* was produced the Association was deeply involved in publishing, safety, hotel inspection and providing members with legal advice. We filmed all their activities and told the story of an organisation which at that time clearly really did care about the interests of its members. The standard of service in every department was extremely high and those involved took a pride in working for the AA and in what they did. Stenson Cooke would have been proud of what they had achieved Today it's a very different story .To many people the

AA has become just another large company owned by venture capitalists whose main aim is to make as much money as possible. Everything has to be profitable. Services have been streamlined or cut and many experienced staff have gone elsewhere. As a result, an organisation which motorists used to trust implicitly and approach for advice,is different today. It is still excellent in many ways but our film recorded the AA in its heyday and I am proud to have been involved in that. A restored digital version of our 1960s film, which marks a milestone in British motoring history and remains interesting to watch, has recently been released on DVD.

Our next venture took me into a new area and involved me in activities most people do not experience in everyday life. I entered the world of organised crime. In the months that followed I became something of an expert in two areas which might have made my fortune if I had approached them in a different way – fraud and shoplifting.

Crime is not the first subject you learn about when you are brought up in a rectory so I got involved rather late in life. I was approached by the security manager of one of Britain's largest credit card companies. I will call him Derek. It is not his real name but as he still holds an important job as security advisor to an international group his real identity cannot be revealed. Derek knew we made films and had seen of our work. He also explained that he had a problem and there were a couple of people he would like me to meet. One of them I was told had spent much of his life behind bars. He had started his career with burglary and housebreaking and then, as he explained when we met, had "graduated to credit card fraud." He was a good looking man. Well spoken and smartly dressed and not at all the public image of a criminal type. It did not take long to realize the he was quite a bright guy. Like many who turn to crime, he never knew his father. When his mother wandered off he was taken into care and ended up in prison where he learned the skills he required. When I first met him he was thirty four. Two years earlier he had decided to reform and move away from crime and back to his girlfriend and daughter who had grown up without him while he was locked away. He had managed to settle down and had recently been offered a job on the right side of the law working for the credit card company that had approached me.

The second man Derek introduced me to had acquired a different set of skills. His expertise was shoplifting. Over the years he had built up a network of contacts who worked as a team which cost shops and stores many thousands of pounds. As far as I am aware he had not reformed but was simply "taking a break" when we were introduced. He had decided to "earn a few bob by tipping the wink" on a couple of recent jobs which he claimed he had heard abut but not been involved in. He seemed a likeable fellow, as many crooks are, but I would not have left my wallet unattended when he was around.

Both these guys played an important part in teaching me all about the subjects I was to explore my next film.

It was a week later at the card company's headquarters that Derek told me about the problem he had mentioned when we first met. His job was to reduce fraud and theft. Organised crime was costing his company millions of pounds a year. He worked in partnership with of a number of retail groups who shared similar objectives. Together they had decided that they wanted us to make a film to help in their quest. They wanted to show how shoplifters work and reduce the ever increasing amount of credit card fraud. I was given a free had as to how the film should be made and a budget which reflected the amount of work involved. I immediately started work on what was to be one of the most interesting projects we had been involved in for some time.

I had to learn to think like a crook so I could write a script which would be interesting and get the right points across. I watched shop assistants at work in various towns and learned how much easier it is to steal something when staff are chatting to each other and not watching what is going on. I saw a girl lift a rack full of baby clothes and hide them in a pram and in the same store watched a young man put a clock in his pocket and stroll casually away. I discovered why thieves often work in teams. One person causes a distraction while another picks up whatever is required. Shoplifting is a huge industry and I was able to learn how it works in practice and how much it ultimately costs us all.

I then went on to learn about credit card fraud. Today fraud has been reduced by using chip and pin cards. Computer technology is much more advanced than it was when our film was made but many of the problems we had to deal with then are still relevant today. Now a card can be read by an electronic device which checks its authenticity in a few seconds. If it has been stolen or has been reported missing it can be invalidated instantly and anyone who is trying to use it may be detained. When our film was made, if you used a credit card you had to sign a voucher which contained a printed impression of the card and worked rather like a cheque. Shop assistants were taught to check the name and the number on the card and to make sure it was not out of date. If their suspicions were aroused in any way they then had to telephone the credit card company using a special code to see if the customer really was who he or she was claiming to be. It took a while but it worked if the assistants were alert and the same is true today.

Now computers can carry out a whole range of security checks but there are still plenty of crooks around and quite a lot of people who are stupid enough to keep their pin numbers and cards in the same place. Staff still need to be alert and if they are in doubt they should still always check. At our sponsor's headquarters over ten thousand credit card transactions were being checked by hand every day when we made our film. We took audiences behind the scenes and showed them how that was done. We then we reminded them of the importance of following the correct security procedures. We did that by re-staging a number of real life incidents. There was the man with a bandaged hand who explained he had recently caught his fingers in a lawn mower so his signature might not look quite right when he signed a cheque. It didn't look right but a shrewd shop assistant had already checked and found the card had been stolen a few days before. Another incident we reconstructed included involved a young man who bought an expensive television and paid for it with his card.

A sales assistant checked the name on the card and made sure it was not out of date. He also noticed that the cardholder was a lieutenant colonel. The man who was using it to buy a television could not have been more than twenty years old. That card too had been stolen.

The third incident we included was the one I liked the most. We reconstructed it as it had occurred. It had happened late at night in an outer London suburb. A drunken man had staggered into an off licence, pointed to a bottle of the most expensive whisky and announced in a slurred voice "I'm going to buy that!" The shop assistant's suspicions were immediately aroused. When his customer added "And I want at least two of them" and produced a credit card to pay for them he carried out the security checks he had been trained to perform. The card had stolen a week before and the police were called. When they arrived to make an arrest they asked what had made the assistant suspicious. He laughed and explained that he knew something was wrong when he looked at the card. The drunk was clearly Irish and the name on the card was obviously not his. There was no way he could be Lee Ho Fook!

WHAT DO THEY TAKE YOU FOR? proved so successful that we were commissioned to make two more films on similar themes. They were both interesting projects and worked so well that they are still being used today. As business increased we found we were getting requests to make films on subjects which were not nearly as interesting and required a great deal of effort to bring them to life. They paid the bills and enabled us to keep the inland revenue in the style to which they appeared to have become accustomed. They also left me with a longing to be able to film subjects which did not require so much work to stop them being dull. With that in mind I decided it was time to for us to produce our own television programmes. At that time almost everything shown on television was produced or commissioned by the major TV networks or bought from Hollywood. Independent productions were almost unheard of. The big companies had contacts, money and resources. We had enthusiasm, ideas and very little else. I knew that expanding at this point could be courting disaster but I am afraid I didn't care. It was time for a change. And that is why I went back to television, this time as my own boss.

BACK TO TELEVISION

At the time when the events you are going about to hear about actually took place, the BBC had around twenty one thousand permanent staff employees. We had five and we had only been in business for just a few years. I mention these facts to give you some idea of the competition we faced. The independent television companies were getting well established. Their commercial strength and their power was matched, if not surpassed, by the television networks of most other countries. For any project of ours to be commercially viable, we knew that we would have to do what they could all do themselves and do it a way which was good enough to encourage them to buy it from us. That meant it had to be better or different from anything they could produce themselves, and that was quite a challenge. Most areas of programming had to be ruled out from the start. We could not afford them. Costume dramas or shows that needed large casts or lots of expensive sets were clearly out the question. As we were not sufficiently inspired to make religious programmes we realised that we were left with very little choice. We could make documentaries or try to find something else we could manage on the limited sums we thought we could raise. Ideas for a number of documentaries were carefully considered and their commercial potential was then assessed. It is interesting to note that the subjects we considered then have now all been produced by other companies. We wanted to take a behind-the-scenes look at London airport and to make a series of shows about antiques. Both ideas were dismissed because we were told they would be impossible to sell. How times have changed!
For weeks I tried to think of something we could do with the limited resources we had at that time. The formula we eventually decided to adopt came to me as an indirect

result of a journey on a train. I was traveling south in an overcrowded carriage. The man sitting next to me was blind and his enormous guide dog had gone to sleep on my feet so I was unable to move and remained anchored to my seat. To make it worse, the dog had fleas. It wasn't much fun and I rather envied a lady opposite me who was reading a book. She smiled all the time and then, quite suddenly, she started to shake with laughter. Tears ran down her cheeks as her whole body shook with mirth. Other people in the carriage then started to share the fun. There is nothing more infectious than laughter. When she eventually regained control I had to ask what she had found so funny. She passed me her book and pointed to the paragraph she had just been reading. It was very funny. The book was called *THE MOON'S A BALLOON* and it was written by an actor who was then at the peak of his career - David Niven.

When I got off the train I started to think. I bought a copy of that book and found myself captivated by the way it had been written. Here was a book written by a man with a good story to tell, who knew how to write. I had seen him on television a few weeks before, being interviewed by one of those personalities who likes to take equal star billing and interrupts great stories at every point. In the book Niven was able to tell his stories without interruption. I found myself wondering if it would be possible to make a television chat show along similar lines. It would not be easy but could it be done? I started to work things out and eventually devised a formula which I thought might work. That was the first step but with our limited resources could we afford to take what would inevitably be a huge risk?

It is one thing to think up new ways of doing a television chat show, and quite another to make those ideas work. When big television companies want to interview a famous personality they pick up a phone, agree a fee and then use one of their fully equipped studios for a couple of hours. I wanted to get away from the restrictions of a studio. The fact that we did not have one may have influenced that decision, but I also believed people would be more relaxed and perform better in less formal surroundings. The big problem was selecting people who we felt we might ask to take part. Most of the names we considered had already appeared on all the usual chat shows. I realised that I would have to approach them with very little to offer, and try to persuade them to do what they probably did not want to do, all over again. It was going to be hard.

We needed people who had a good story to tell, and that meant they would probably already be well know. Television viewers want star personalities with big names. They are not likely to be enthralled by the revelations of Mr Boreveryone from Eastbourne or Mrs Saiditall from Penge. I spent days I making lists of people I thought we might approach and eventually decided to start at the top.

David Niven's book had been at the top of the bestseller's list around the world for months. He had always been a popular actor. He had starred in numerous films and given millions of people a lot of pleasure. For his efforts as an actor he won an Oscar. He had also managed to remain gainfully employed throughout his long career and that is an achievement which most actors can only dream about. To me, and to the millions who saw his films and read his books, he was unquestionably a major star. It was therefore an act of total folly for anyone in the position I was in then to even think about asking him to take part in our proposed chat show.

Fortunately, when it comes to folly, my efforts are frequently unsurpassed!

It took me three days to make the call. Three days trying to sum up the courage to telephone a major star. It had taken even longer to discover his ex-directory number. For hour after hour I wondered what I would encounter

when I made that call and what I would say if I ever got through. Eventually I found myself dialling the number. It was quickly answered by one of Niven's staff. He spoke French and, with my schoolboy command of that language, the task I faced was clearly going to get off to a doubtful start. After quite a long discussion he asked me to hold the line and then disappeared. Several minutes passed and I was beginning to think I had been cut off when Niven himself came on the line.
I had already decided that there was only one way to handle the situation I now found myself in. I had to be completely honest and see how things went from there. I explained that I had started a small film company five years ago and immediately made clear that it was not like the companies he dealt with every day. I summed up the difference in a couple of words. They had everything. We had nothing. At first, I am afraid, I did all the talking. The silence from the other end made me wonder if we had been cut off. Fortunately we had not. Niven then asked me some questions which I tried to answer. I told him about the girl on the train who had been reading his book. He laughed and the conversation continued for quite a long time. Eventually I managed to ask if he would be prepared to see me if I went to meet him near his home in France. Much to my delight, he said that he would. We agreed a time and date and ended the call.
For a long time I sat in my Covent Garden office, wondering if the conversation I had just been involved in had really taken place. He had sounded so nice and so completely genuine. Were we really going to meet, or was it an illusion? I looked down at my diary and saw that I had scribbled a date and a time. Now I could only hope.
On the agreed date I found myself on an aircraft landing in Nice. I was the last to leave the plane, having by now convinced myself that I was on a fool's errand. I was about to find that no one knew anything about any

appointment and Niven would probably be away. I walked into the airport building. By now most of the other passengers had left. I showed my passport to a man at the gate and moved on. The main concourse was almost empty as I approached a line of taxis which were waiting outside. I had not gone far when I heard a voice.
"Would your name be Burder?"
I turned and found myself facing a man with a large hat pulled down across his face. I confirmed my name. The hat was raised and I came face to face with David Niven. I did not know then, and I do not know now, why such A successful star bothered to come and meet me personally. He could have sent any of his minions but, as I was to discover in the next few weeks, Niven was not like that. He was genuine to the core. He told me, as we drove off to lunch (which, incidentally he insisted on paying for) that our telephone chat had been a refreshing change. I had made him laugh and taken him back to his own early days. We got on well and in the weeks that followed I had the chance to get to know a man who had already given the world so much pleasure. After lunch at a tiny and excellent restaurant right on the sea in Nice, we drove to his home at Cap Ferrat where we talked all afternoon. I told him what I wanted to do and asked what he thought about our proposed new format. He told me that he never went to see any of his films. If that rule could remain unbroken, he felt sure it would be fine. We agreed what to film and we set a date. He and I would sit in his garden and chat about his life and views. I explained that only one side of the conversation would ever be used. The format I planned would enable me to cut out my questions. Only he would appear on screen and it would thus be only his voice audiences would hear. We put the plan into action over the following weeks and ended up with a permanent record of Niven at his best. A record of a born raconteur who is completely relaxed and enjoying himself in his own surroundings.

In the cutting rooms the film went together better than even I had ever dared to hope. The new format really worked and the film came to life. I showed our final edited version to a friend who worked for one of the big television networks. He loved it and said he thought it was just the sort of thing companies like his were always looking for.

For a moment I thought we had arrived, but then he added: " Of course, we can't take it on its own. We could only buy a series. We need eight or twelve programmes before we can allocate a slot."

We were almost back to square one.

It took us months to decide what we should do next. I wanted to make more television shows, but Britain was in the middle of a three-day working week as a result of series of disputes between the unions and the government. When we started our business Harold Wilson was Prime Minister. He was an uninspiring leader and for months interest rates hovered around sixteen percent! It was an uphill struggle for anyone to trade profitably and a terrible time start a new business. We did not want to borrow money because interest rates were so high. We realised we could lose what we had so far managed to make by expanding too fast and trying to finance a television series which needed far more resources than we at that time could provide.

After a lot of thought we decided to see if we could raise some capital by making some more industrial training films. The ones we made did quite well and eventually gave us enough money make some more television shows. We already had our Niven programme which other potential subjects were able to see. As everyone seemed to like it, the task of persuading others to get involved became a lot easier. I eventually produced a short list of five top people. They were different ages and had very different views, but they all had interesting stories to tell and they were stories I felt we could present very well. I called the first person on that list the following day. She had just arrived in London from the USA. For many years she had been a major Hollywood star. Her career had almost become part of film history. When I met her in her suite at Claridges hotel she had not made a film for several years, but her earlier achievements were such that she was still a very big name. It turned into a rather depressing day.

As she talked about here life it soon became clear that as the years had passed she had became very bitter. She had worked with a host of other big stars but did not have a good word to say about anyone. She was so full of herself, and so unpleasant about everyone else, that I was eventually forced to the conclusion that any appearance she might make in our new series would be likely to remain on the shelf and prove impossible to sell.

The person we eventually chose to be the subject of of our second film was as unlike that lady as anyone could be. I first met him at the United Nations building in Geneva. It takes around twenty minutes to walk from one end of that building to the other. As we strolled along, I asked him why he did so much voluntary work for the United Nations Children's Fund. His reply neatly summarised his deeply held views.

"The nations of the world spend the same amount on children every year as they do on arms every two hours. That's enough to get me interested. I think it is scandalous. It is also very short-sighted. Even if you are a hawk it seems to me to be madness to spend so much on the cannons and so little on the fodder."

With such a human approach to life, you may perhaps think that I was in the company of a full-time UN official, whose life had been dedicated to providing human aid. In fact I had joined an actor who also wrote books and directed operas films and plays. He had been a top International star for years but remained a delightfully modest man, who made people happy wherever he went.

His name as Peter Ustinov.
A few months before our first meeting, I had watched Peter play the lead in a major American television show. It was being transmitted to a massive audience live from coast to coast. He was playing the part of the great Doctor Johnson - a performance which was to win him an Emmy award - a point he was too modest to mention when he first met Instead he started to apologise for what I had seen and tell me why he was unhappy with what he had done.
"It was quite difficult to do because it was all live and we only had a few weeks' rehearsal. A huge lamp burst right behind me just as I had to get out of bed and with bare feet walk across to sign my dictionary. I could see the floor was covered with glass and managed to shuffle through pushing it aside, but that wasn't the only problem. Everyone praised my restraint in the death scene, but I couldn't really do otherwise because my make up was
coming apart!"
When Ustinov was young his father wanted him to be a lawyer. He had other views and explained that he wanted to be an actor which he felt was really "the same profession but much less dangerous to my fellow men." Fortunately he managed to fulfil his ambition and we were thus been able to enjoy his many talents.
Peter was the second name on the list of people I wanted to feature in our shows. He had already made many appearances for the major networks, but again I felt he would be happier working in a less formal environment, with people who were not likely to dictate the content or pace of his contribution to the show. It was a bold assumption which subsequently proved correct. When introductions were first made, I was again completely honest. I explained how we worked and emphasised that, compared to the companies he normally worked with, we were about the size of a pebble on the

beach. By then our Niven programme had been completed. Niven and Ustinov had worked together on many occasions and were great friends. I suspect they may have discussed the situation. When I approached him Peter agreed to appear in our show and we began what was to be an unforgettable experience for everyone involved.

There was only one problem anyone who worked with Peter Ustinov needed to be aware of. You had to be ready to laugh, so much and so often that it could become quite painful. He was wonderful company. We shot our film at several locations. Most of it was filmed at his private retreat in the Balearic Islands. I will not reveal the exact location, as I have no wish to abuse his hospitality or to allow others to follow as I believe he never allowed anyone else to film there. We also visited his old school – Westminster. When he was a pupil there attitudes to education were very different from those prevalent today. He once told an audience of diplomats that in his view a British education was "the best in the world, if you survived it. If you don't there is nothing left but the diplomatic corps."

At Westminster he was expected to wear a top hat, a tailcoat and carry a rolled umbrella. The school prospectus explained that this was in order to differentiate the boys from city messengers who also used umbrellas. As most of the messengers were over sixty Peter told me that he thought that note was rather a waste of time.

We filmed our main discussion in two days as the sun shone down out of a clear blue sky. Shooting started a day late because our two cameras and crates of other equipment were impounded at the airport. A militant official refused to accept documents stamped with a stamp which had proved perfectly acceptable everywhere else for at least ten years. As we waited to start filming, I asked Peter how he had first met and become friends with David Niven. We were later able to capture his hilarious explanation in our film and it has thus been preserved for posterity.

The war was at its height. Niven and Ustinov were both involved but in very different ways. Peter was a army private – the most junior rank of all. David was a colonel. He had been trained at Sandhurst and knew what army life was all about . Ustinov was never cut out to be a soldier and his first experiences in uniform had not encouraged him. He recalled how on one occasion as part of an exercise, his unit was ordered to attack the town of Maidstone, to test the effectiveness of the home guard there. Peter managed to detach himself from his unit and by using tactics which he thought were shrewd, arrived in Maidstone ahead of the other troops. On his arrival he came face to face with the head of the defending army – a colonel in the home guard. As it was only an exercise, Ustinov shouted " Bang!" at the colonel, who stubbornly refused to die. The umpire responsible for refereeing the exercise was then called. He had a terrible stutter and told the Colonel "You're d-d-d-d-dead sir," but the old man still refused to die.

The matter was only resolved when Peter was sent back to his own unit. What happened then as also explored in our film.

During their army years Ustinov and Niven were persuaded to make a training film in which they would both appear. To cope with their difference in rank, Ustinov was appointed to be Niven's batman, for which he was paid fourteen shillings a week! The film they made was called *THE WAY AHEAD*, and he described its production in hilarious detail in the course of our programme. Filming proceeded at a good steady pace. We knew what we wanted and he was of an Oscar winning performer who knew all the tricks required to bring every scene to life. He told me that it was a relief working with people who knew what was required as in the last film he had made work had been held up for days by a dispute

between two so called "experts" who had been called to advise.
He was playing the part of a Dutch priest and two real priests had then been employed as technical advisors. They were at loggerheads with each other from day one. They did not like to be on the set at the same time so, when Peter was acting, one of them would come along and say, " What is he doing without a cross?"
They would then provide a cross and shoot the scene again.
The first priest would then go off to the canteen and advisor
number two would come along. He would then ask
" Why is he wearing a cross? No Dutch priest
would ever wear a cross in a situation like that."
In the end everything had to be shot two ways and Peter was quietly able to double his income.
With stories like that, you can imagine how quickly the time passed when we were filming! We finished our interview and went off to shoot at other locations. The film was then edited and completed about seven weeks after work on it had started.
I contacted Peter when he visited London a few weeks later and asked if he would like to see the result of our efforts. He said he would, and he came to the only Viewing facility we had at that time – a projector and a small screen on the fourth floor of our Covent Garden headquarters. His reactions were a pleasure to watch. He made some helpful comments and said he had enjoyed what he had seen. As he was a totally honest man, I am sure that he did. We were honoured that he had agreed to take part and show so much interest in what, from his point of view, must have been the smallest show on earth.
We had now sponsored and produced two of our own television programmes both of which were well received whenever they were shown. To complete a series we needed to make at least six more. Money was steadily

coming but we found ourselves under pressure to make more training films. There were companies waiting to pay us good money if we would make training films for them. We decided to make two more television shows and then return to industrially sponsored work where there was clearly money to be made and a growing demand for our services.

The two TV shows we made starred two very different characters. Both were very successful in their chosen careers, but one had been working much longer than the other. I wanted to ensure that the shows we made would appeal to people of all ages. We had so far featured two characters who had been at the top for years. They were, quite simply, the best you can get, and I knew that it was going to be difficult to maintain such a high standard. We had to find others who had been successful enough to have a good story to tell. They also needed to have enough personality and command of words to be able to put their views across in our newly devised format.

The next artiste we chose had done relatively few television appearances. I had been told that his singing and dancing was superb, but without an orchestra he would probably be lost and would refuse to do anything at all. It was a verdict we were soon able to disprove for the man we approached proved to be very good on his own. In our programme he broke new ground and gave one of the best performances of his life. His name was Tommy Steele
. At the start of his career, like the Beatles, Tommy was besieged by thousands of fans who regarded him as one of the biggest names in the newly emerging world of pop music. I first met him at his London home – a smart listed mansion, which he and his wife had furnished in excellent taste. As we sat and chatted about the film we were planning, I could not help marveling at what such a relatively young man had managed to achieve. He had

been born as Tommy Hicks in one of the poorest parts of London. His parents had no connections at all with any of the arts. His first job was as a ship's steward, where he had many hilarious adventures which he recalled in our film. When he was at sea he borrowed a guitar from his ship's cook and taught himself to play. He started "messing around with tunes" and eventually came ashore to try and earn some money.

In London Tommy joined a group of young lads who called themselves "The Vipers." They made a cheerful noise but not much cash and were about to disband when Steele was spotted by a photographer who was to change his life. Her explained that he wanted to become Steele's manager as he felt he was "star material." As he had never managed anyone else before and Steele had only performed in coffee bars for a few weeks, his enthusiasm was difficult to understand. Tommy was still under 21 years of age, so his mother had to be asked to sign his first contract. When the photographer explained his ambitions for her son, Mrs Hicks listened patiently and then gave her verdict.

"If he is not a star in two weeks, he will go back to sea!" What happened next has become an important part of pop music history.

In our programme, which was largely filmed at Tommy's London home, he relaxed and proved to be an excellent raconteur. He told us how the Queen Mother had saved him from "a fate worse than death" during a Royal Command Performance and he talked about his success as star of the stage and screen versions of the smash hit musical *HALF A SIXPENCE*. He also spoke movingly about his close friendship with Walt Disney, recalling conversations in which Disney had confided in him, on condition that the issues they discussed would not be revealed until after his death.

As filming proceeded Tommy told me what it had been like when as a young man he had been rehearsing on stage, with the great Oscar Hammerstein sitting in the stalls. He also described a wild New York party, where the guest of honour was Princess Margaret and a major Hollywood star had got so drunk he collapsed in front of her. The whole film was great fun and a worthy addition to our ever growing series.

I had been warned in advance that the next person we proposed to film was "a real horror," and that prediction proved to be correct as he was always the first to admit. Vincent Price was undoubtedly the king of horror movies. As we were to learn, he was equally successful in a number of other areas.

We filmed much of our Vincent Price programme at the Royal Pavilion In Brighton. It is a city I have had the pleasure of being associated with for many years. The Royal Pavilion I s one of its most endearing attractions. It was built for the Prince Regent in 1874. It seemed to be an appropriate place to film Vincent Price because he made his stage debut playing The Prince in a play called Victoria Regina. Before that he had worked briefly as a museum guide and as a gigolo in a Viennese nightclub. Like many big stars, he never intended to get into films. As a young man he studied fine arts at Yale and later took a masters degree In London. His time at Yale ended at the height of the depression. Three close friends committed suicide not because they were in trouble but because their fathers had lost all their money! Price told me he could never understand why it was the sons who committed suicide and not their fathers.

We spent one of our days filming in the Royal Pavilion's kitchen. It's a huge room, designed to enable teams of cooks to prepare vast meals for hundreds of people. Price was in his element. He was himself an accomplished chef. As the cameras rolled he recalled a thanksgiving dinner he had organised and cooked for some VIP guests. When the time came for dinner to be served he discovered he had forgotten to turn on the oven.

The turkey remained uncooked until most of the guests were too drunk to care! Price was world-famous for his acting but there was another aspect to his life which did not get so much publicity. When he went on the stage, the fine art qualifications he had acquired at Yale were not forgotten. He remained interested in the arts until the end of his days. At one point he worked as a consultant to the American retail giant, Sears Roebuck. In our film he recalled how they gave him a budget of what today would be millions of dollars, to purchase works of art which would help to educate the nation.

On screen Price's performances will always fascinate. In the course of our discussions I began to appreciate just how much work he put into every role he played. He explained why he loved playing villains.

"Heroes are just all smiles and a mouth full of teeth. Villains are much more fun!

As our filming proceeded Price recalled his experiences of working with many of the world's most famous directors.

There was Cecil B De Mille who felt that "any amount of money was worth it if you cold see it on the screen." Howard Hughes gave him a part in *THE SON OF SINBAD*, which Price thought was "one of the worst films ever made." At first he was unable to understand how anyone could finance it. He then noticed that the script featured hundreds of pretty girls all of whom were under contract to Howard Hughes and "this dreadful film gave them an excuse the make their first and probably only screen appearance!"

Perhaps Price's most revealing comments were about Errol Flynn. He and Flynn had starred together in two disastrous films. On the first occasion, Flynn did not bother to learn his lines and made them up as he went along. On the second, he had arrived to start filming six weeks late! Our production proved to be rather less chaotic. We completed the main scenes and returned to

London.
I wanted to make more television shows to complete our series but events at home obliged us to halt our activities. To complete the series I envisaged we would have needed to borrow quite large sums of money and bank interest rates were rising to an all-time high. Waiting to go on screen we had lined up some of the biggest names of the day. They had seen the shows we had completed and were keen to take part in what was beginning to be regarded as a pretty good series. It was a nice position to be in, but one indisputable fact remained. We were then still young people running a very new company. We could borrow money to make more shows but at that time Britain was in the middle of a depression and interest rates were spiralling out of control. There was no guarantee that anything we might borrow could ever be repaid. The series had been my idea and I had to decide its future. We could settle for the shows we had already made and sell them on a one off basis or gamble and make some more. It was one of the hardest decisions I have ever had to make. In the end I chose the safest way and until the world economic scene brightened, our television production plans were temporarily shelved.
When I returned to my office I wondered if people would ask us to make enough films to let us to continue to pay the bills. On that score at least, I need not have worried. From that day on I have never needed to look for work. For fifty years our clients have proved how wonderful and loyal they are. In their service we have shot films on a huge range of different subjects. Recent productions include films on fires In prisons and on Europe's largest air cargo operation. That proved to be particularly rewarding. It was sponsored by one of Europe's biggest airlines and it took us three years to complete. The work was considerably extended because the airline's main contractor had a dispute with

its main sub contractor half way through the work. They decided to sue each other and the whole project was held up for months while they tried to resolve their differences in court. We were about the only people to actually benefit from that enormous project. When the law suits began we were employed by both sides to provide video evidence to show how much work had actually been done. The legal arguments went on for months and were able to smile all the way to the bank.

In this book I have deliberately concentrated on the early years on our business because for me they were the most fun but we have gone a long way from there . As the business has grown I have travelled round the world many times and produced films which are currently being used in 27 countries. I have just checked the first copy of one of our latest training production. - The Common Sense Guide to Manual Handling - in Mandarin Chinese! Twenty years after our Niven /Ustinov/ Price and Steele television programmes were temporarily set aside, I decided to dig them out of the vaults and take a fresh look at them. With hindsight I wanted to see if they were as good as people who saw them when they were originally produced had said they were. We had moved offices several times since the films were first made. In the intervening years the film laboratory, which had processed and retained all the original material, had been bought out by another firm. Their premises had been demolished and many films appeared to have been lost at that time. For months I tried to trace the negatives of our shows. I knew they contained a wealth of unique material and could not bring myself to believe that it had all been lost for ever. For years my efforts were un-rewarded and then, when I had almost given up hope, they were found in some boxes which had been dumped in a garage. Months have subsequently been spent digitally restoring everything we found. It has been a difficult task and an expensive one but the end result has more than justified the efforts of all those involved. Four classic films have now been restored and digitally updated and will again be available for the world to enjoy.

A few months ago I was asked to give the address at a memorial service for one of the masters who taught me at Milton Abbey school over fifty years ago. Bruce Coleman was a wonderful man. When I first met him I was thirteen and he had just started his teaching career. He was one of the youngest and ablest members of staff. He survived trying to teach me French and went on to encourage generations of boys to fulfil their own particular aims and ambitions.

As I stood in the abbey church that day and looked down at the congregation which filled every available space, I again realised how lucky I have been. In the front row below me I could see Bruce's sons and grandsons - the next generation waiting for a cue to take their place centre stage in the drama of life. I hope that they, and any other young people who may read this book, will find something they really want to do and then enjoy doing it for the rest of their lives. I thank God every day for the many blessings I have received. Now the next generation must take the helm and steer the ship of life into new waters. I wish them well!

ARCHIVE FILMS ON DVD

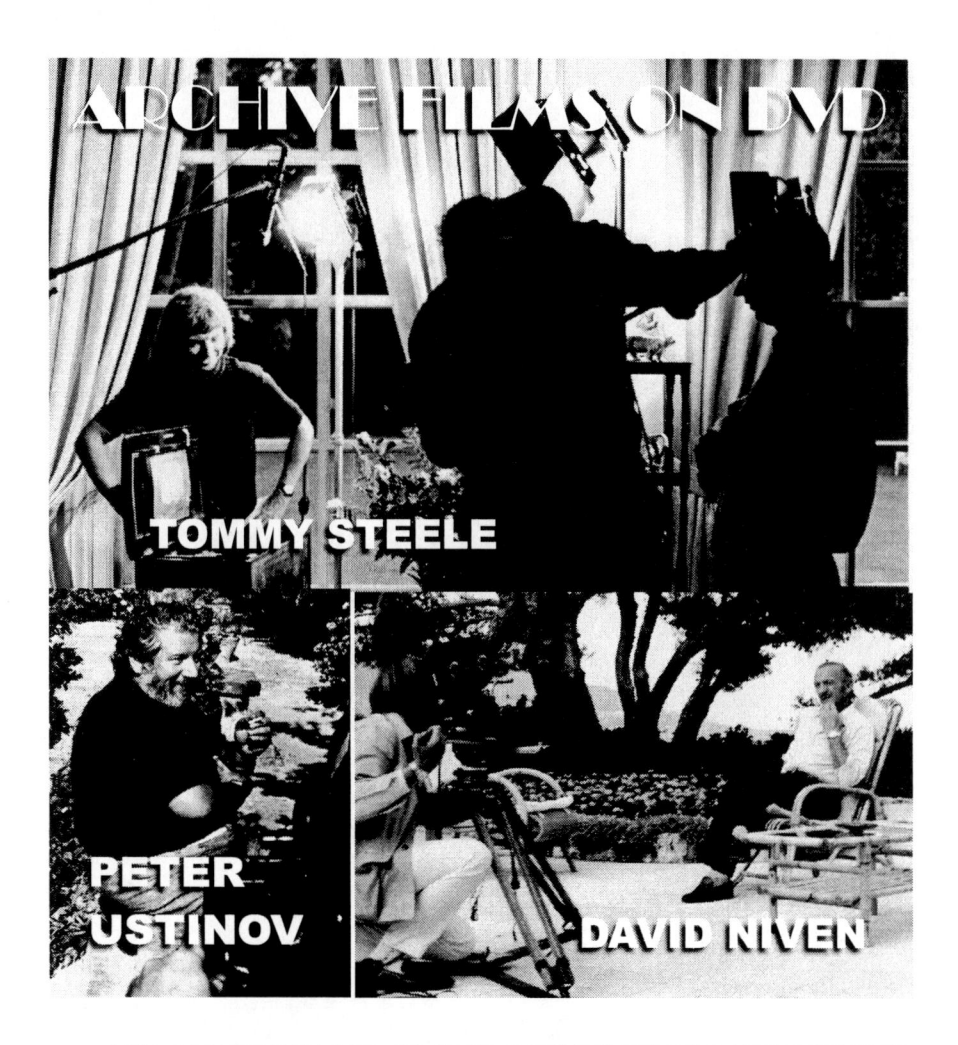

TOMMY STEELE

PETER USTINOV

DAVID NIVEN

AND MANY OF THE OTHER PRODUCTIONS MENTIONED
IN THIS BOOK ARE NOW AVAILABLE ON DVD

**FOR DETAILS CONTACT
BURDERFILMS@AOL.COM**

MORE ARCHIVE FILMS ON DVD

GUERNSEY - ECHOES OF THE PAST

BOURNEMOUTH - SOMETHING FOR EVERYONE

AA - THE SIGN FOR SERVICE

MAIDEN VOYAGE ON ORIANA

MILTON ABBEY 2005

FOR DETAILS CONTACT
BURDERFILMS@AOL.COM